Also by Debbie Raymond and Bonnie Meroth

THE GROWTH OF TRUTH

INTENTIONAL SPIRITS

VOICES FROM THE TITANIC

BONNIE MEROTH AND DEBBIE RAYMOND

BALBOA.
PRESS

A DIVISION OF HAY HOUSE

Balboa Press books may be ordered through booksellers or by contacting:

Balboa Press
A Division of Hay House
1663 Liberty Drive
Bloomington, IN 47403
www.balboapress.com
1 (877) 407-4847

Because of the dynamic nature of the Internet, any web addresses or links contained in
this book may have changed since publication and may no longer be valid. The views
expressed in this work are solely those of the author and do not necessarily reflect the views
of the publisher, and the publisher hereby disclaims any responsibility for them.

The author of this book does not dispense medical advice or prescribe the use of any technique as a form of
treatment for physical, emotional, or medical problems without the advice of a physician, either directly or
indirectly. The intent of the author is only to offer information of a general nature to help you in your quest
for emotional and spiritual well-being. In the event you use any of the information in this book for yourself,
which is your constitutional right, the author and the publisher assume no responsibility for your actions.

Any people depicted in stock imagery provided by Thinkstock are models,
and such images are being used for illustrative purposes only.
Certain stock imagery © Thinkstock.

Printed in the United States of America.

ISBN: 978-1-4525-8402-7 (sc)
ISBN: 978-1-4525-8403-4 (e)

Library of Congress Control Number: 2013918194

Balboa Press rev. date: 10/17/2013

To the Living we owe respect, but to the dead we owe the truth.

Voltaire

INTRODUCTION

I have never ceased to experience the wonder when I open my intuitive room to the Other Side. Even though I can not fully comprehend what I see, hear and smell in witnessing the existence of life in the unknown, I see those who have died and I faithfully receive what is being brought to me. Those who wait patiently to share their stories must also faithfully accept the same—what I can give to them.

My verbatim visions from the victims of the Titanic are printed in this book in Bookman style bold font. We clarified their stories with modern vernacular to avoid misinterpretation or conjecture about their actual messages then printed the transposed texts in italics to differentiate each the original and the clarified version.

As these spirits of the Titanic accepted my invitation to come and speak, I shared their stories with them, listening to how the victims regretfully drowned and how they now live on from a sunken wreck in the ocean depths.

It is a journey only for those who wish to come along.

Debbie Raymond

CONTENTS

PROLOGUE

The bottom of the bathtub blurred and she realized it was filling with water. Knowing the drain was not plugged, she watched as the water level rose higher and higher. Nearly a foot deep, the surface changed to a smooth wooden floor. Still kneeling, she saw that her tub was completely gone and she was scrubbing what had become the wooden planks of a wide deck. Shiny black high boots stood in front of her. Laced tightly to their tops, they met neatly pressed dark navy britches. Her eyes followed the pants up to the ashen face of a young man.

Cold penetrated her bones. Drips from his loose soaked clothes hit her, biting in as harshly as the air that had changed to briny and frigid in the warmth of the bathroom. Above her, an ice blue sky replaced the white ceiling and she knew she was in another place. Her contemporary surroundings were gone, and she with them.

She now kneeled on a huge ship—no, an ocean liner she corrected herself—in the middle of the ocean. Dead silence stood between her and the male form. As she stared at him, she realized he had the sunken eyes of someone who had not slept in a hundred years. His flesh held a bluish tinge and his purple lips did not move. Leaning from her knees onto the back of her calves, she looked around. A restless crowd of people milled on the deck and surrounded her in a cacophony of voices speaking to each other, but not to her. They did not realize she was there.

Skirt hems brushed across the top of her thighs. She looked up at the aloof faces under huge hats of the women in Edwardian dress. Obviously, they were of high society and their snobbery came through as clear as a bell. The tragic young man alone, who was evidently not of their social station, was showing her a memory from his time on earth. Only he was sharing these moments from long ago, as was the way with spirits.

CHAPTER 1

THE NEW PROJECT

"Not everyone is at peace . . . ."

The whisper woke me from a deep sleep.

Rolling toward the nightstand, I looked at the softly lit digital face of my trusty 30-year-old old radio alarm clock that showed 3:00 a.m.

Bewitching hour, so it was said, a time when the spirits came out for some reason or another. I must have been deep in a dream. Well, not anymore. I was wide awake with just enough sleep so I could not fall back into it with ease, but not enough to jump out of bed ready for the day either. I hated when then happened.

Sharing its light through the window, the moon was hanging full enough to define the items on top of the nightstand. Lying on my left side, I freed my arm from the stack of blankets under the feather puff and groped for the right button to turn on the radio before settling onto my back. Not remembering everything I dreamed, that haunting voice from my sleep echoed in my head as the volume dial turned to a louder tone. Forgetting what I dreamt was not unusual. Sometimes I remembered, sometimes not. Sometimes I could not remember why I walked into another room. I hated when that happened, too.

The auto tune on the radio was set to a favorite overnight FM talk show. This night, the subject matter was ghosts. Of course, it was. It was just after 3:00 a.m.

"Not all dead people rest peacefully."

Seriously.

That got my attention and I knew it did not come from a dream. It came from the radio as a statement from a psychic medium guest of the program. All remote thoughts of going back to sleep were gone. For the next two hours, my mind was engrossed listening to callers as they asked questions that elicited answers they mostly wanted to hear. Some responses brought joy, some pain and tears, but all seemed to bring closure of some sort and it was interesting to hear how many people needed to know that loved ones rested in peace and even more fascinating to hear about those who did not rest in peace.

I was easily relating to all this because my last few months of working with a psychic medium writing her memoir tuned me into the paranormal. The Other Side was becoming a normal daily thing for me to deal with, as normal as it could be. This psychic was always surrounded by spirits and easily communicated with them. In the beginning, it seemed almost a "let's pretend" thing, especially when she said they were in the room with us. It was definitely not pretend. When I facetiously agreed to be her ghost writer, the pun became the provenance of a whole new very real other world.

Ironically, Debbie would be at my house in a few hours to discuss a new project and she was going to love hearing my story about the talk show. Living in the world of the paranormal, she could more than relate and refreshingly, the guest, callers and host on this program were all on the same level of believing that there was another dimension out there somewhere called the Other Side. Too often, there were rude skeptics. Well, they would know enough someday when their time came, I thought while throwing off the blankets and king-sized puff ready to start the day.

Four hours later, with a five-mile walk, a bit of gardening, a couple of loads of laundry, bookkeeping, vacuuming and morning ablutions behind me, I scrunched my damp hair trying to organize blonde short curls that would never be tamed. By mid-morning, it was already near hot and humid—much too soon for early spring—and my hair would have its way. Debating whether or not to turn on the air conditioning and deciding against it, I headed for the kitchen in my bare feet, nicely satisfied that the wait was over for warmer floors after a long freezing New England winter.

After washing my hands and donning a favorite white and blue checked apron, I pulled healthy salad ingredients from the refrigerator for the very early lunch we preferred over breakfast food. Automatically and habitually computing nutrients while pulling hulled raw pumpkin seeds from the pantry to join the produce and all the while pleased they were on the second shelf where they were supposed to be, I felt that spending time looking for things was a waste of precious moments of life. Ten minutes used up on a misplaced item could never be lived over. Everything belonged in a place of easy access, even pumpkin seeds.

Breaking apart leaves of lettuce and musing about the good news of sales from our recently published book, I reminisced about what the past year had brought. It had brought me Debbie and a long contemplative journey learning about what happens when one reaches the Other Side. Personal experiences with clairvoyants who could see things past, present and future was not new to me, but this was my first experience with a medium, people on this earth who not only can see ghosts, but who can communicate with them. Debbie was both psychic and medium and even more. Witnessing all the paranormal stuff over the months had become almost as matter-of-fact to me as it was to her.

Almost.

At times, when we were working together in the same room or on the telephone, apparitions came to her with messages and at times, ghosts would pop in to visit, walking in or floating in or however they perambulated. Only she could see them, of course. For Debbie, it was matter-of-fact and a way of life. At the beginning, the concept was definitely surreal and incredulous. Knowing visible spirits were around her was still a difficult concept for me to grasp if I really thought about it, but it was now a way of life for me, too. Being with Debbie and her spirits became quite nonchalant and very accepting with the fact that she saw the ghosts and I did not.

Glancing up, I gazed out the big window over the kitchen sink and thought it was a post card picture perfect day. Yellow finches sat on the birdbath in my meditation garden. Some perched in the Japanese maple for their turn in the gray granite bowl that no longer held ice. Their recently morphed bright color manifested another indication that winter was over. The huge copper Chinese gong swayed. Strange. There was not a breath of morning breeze. Maybe a larger bird had just flown off the enormous copper sphere, giving it that momentum. No. It would have taken something much heavier than even a flock of large birds to move the eighty pound gong. All at once, it stilled. Even more odd.

Crossing the open-concept width of the house from the kitchen to the mullioned bay window in the living room area, I glanced out to see if a storm front approached. Because the house was on a good-sized hill, the wind would sometimes gust a portent to foul weather, but no clouds headed my way and the sun beamed over the front of the house making my solar chimes on the tiled window seat tinkle.

Debbie had arrived but had yet to turn up the driveway. She was sitting in her car below the hill looking toward the field, a huge area that was split in width with a row of deciduous trees. This morning, the view was striking with the mid-morning sun shining on the beautiful farm land that rolled over the countryside and slipped into a panorama of the mountains to the north. Such a bucolic scene, I mused. No wonder she took a minute to enjoy, even though she was running a bit late. Good for her. Her car sat there for a minute or so before turning sharply to come up the paved driveway edged with sedum already turning green in a ground still cold and groggy from winter.

Parking her treasured eight year old Cadillac in front of one of the two garage bays, she gathered her paraphernalia and headed for the doorway entrance. The motion-activated big plastic green frog next to the garage door croaked and made her jump, as it always did with its sudden deep hoarse noises and she laughed as she also always did. After one push of the Westminster chime door bell, she let herself in and followed the carpeted stairs leading to the kitchen, unnecessarily announcing her arrival with the usual cheery greeting—a big hello.

Back at the kitchen counter finishing the salads, I looked around and smiled at her, noticing that in spite of the warm morning, she wore her favorite red sweatshirt. Her long light brown curls were as unruly as my shorter ones. We had that in common and much more, compatible with our philosophies of life and what our lives had brought us, but I was old enough to be her mother. I thought myself wise and worldly due to age; I thought her wise and worldly in two worlds because of her gift.

"I just saw a man near the bottom of the driveway staring into your garden out back."

Of course she did.

Of course, I had not.

Debbie described him. "He was elderly and dressed in standard denim overalls over a white shirt with the sleeves pushed up. His eyes were as blue as his cap. They twinkled as he waved to me."

"What did you do?"

"I waved back." She was just so blasé about this everyday occurrence for her. "I figured the spirit was associated with you because he was looking up so intently into one of the gardens in the back yard."

No wonder the gong was moving. Some ghosts could do that.

"I know exactly who it was. Who it is? Was?"

Because Debbie brought those who have passed into the present, I was never quite sure quite how to put it. It was nice to think of this farmer in the present even though he had passed and was on the Other Side.

"He died a few years ago and I bet he was checking out my garden gong. He built the stand that it hangs on. He wouldn't let me give him a penny for it, bless his heart."

This was just one spirit she would experience during the day. A trail of them seemed to follow her everywhere, including to my house where, evidently, I had a few already hanging around. They knew she could see them. At times, it was more than a little disconcerting and sometimes I actually thought I could feel them. That was really disconcerting and, hopefully, mostly just the power of suggestion on my part. I always felt it was necessarily polite for me to accept them without reservation, all of them, the ones who came with Debbie and the ones who were already around me. Thankfully, they seemed to be well-behaved. However, I wasn't taking chances. Being polite to them was the name of the game.

Slicing an avocado to top the salads and considering them culinary accomplishments, I took a moment to admire the combination of colors, textures and flavors before putting them on the bar and announcing that I had a rather unusual idea for a second book.

"Great!"

With no intention for disrespect, I asked what seemed impossible.

"So, can you just call up a spirit?"

"Of course I can."

"But, can you be specific with any particular one?"

"Yes. If they accept my invitation and they want to come and my intentions are good."

My questions were answered, but before we went any deeper in our conversation, Debbie's dark eyes become distant. She had gone to another place, if only for a few seconds. Actually, her traveling off somewhere in time could happen in a split second, a difficult fact to assimilate. Those big beautiful brown eyes frequently glanced away as if in deep thought when she was seeing something or hearing something along the line of a ghost. The distraction was brief most of the time and never seemed rude, but she would definitely go somewhere for a moment and it seemed paramount to her, and to me, that she had to pay attention to something.

Or someone.

She was definitely paying attention to someone else at the moment. When a spirit came in contact with Debbie, she respectfully gave them her full attention and that was what was going down at the moment. I looked around to see if I could sense anything.

Nothing.

"Somebody just came in, huh." The statement was without question in an okay-here-we-go-again tone. It was sort of fine with me. At least I didn't have to make another salad.

Warily looking around, I thought maybe I wasn't dealing that great with it all.

Debbie nodded and said, "She's an elderly lady wearing bobby pins in her gray hair to hold back a bun at her neck. There is a full apron over her dress. She is only about five feet tall and has thick glasses with small round wire lenses."

The description matched my maternal grandmother who had passed twenty years before. Grammy always wore one of those full front aprons with big pockets. Having been close to my grandmother, maybe that was why I liked aprons. Thinking Debbie had an amazing gift and thinking how this was just a little weird and then on second thought a lot weird, I put the extra tomato slices into a plastic container and popped them into the refrigerator. Grabbing a bottle of spring water for each of us, I handed one to Debbie and sitting on a bar stool opposite her at the long counter in my kitchen, tucked my short dress in around my legs.

"Oh. There's a dog lying there." Debbie nodded to the entrance leading from the kitchen to the deck. The sun coming through the French door window panes was warming the scatter rug over the wide beams of the red oak floor. "He looks like the Golden Retriever type and his name has something to do with law enforcement or the armed services or something."

I did not have a dog.

I had not had a dog for nearly fifty years.

I knew it was my Trooper and told Debbie. Contemplating my grandmother and my dog, I could say nothing else. Three personal ghosts were enough. After putting the bowls from lunch in the dishwasher, we grabbed our water bottles and headed up the open wooden staircase to my office to start our new project. My farmer friend, Grammy and Trooper could hang around, but we had work to do.

CHAPTER 2

NOT EVERYONE IS
RESTING PEACEFULLY

D ebbie settled in at her usual four foot long table perpendicular to the work
area on which my computer sat. From that spot, she could see the monitor. My
office belied the intrinsic neatness of the rest of the house. Current projects from
my public relations, sales and marketing company were laid out here and there over
the long tables I preferred to fancy desks. Framed pictures taken over the years in
my photo journalism career spotted the walls around the good-sized room. A fax,
separate phone with answering machine, a desk computer and printer were the only
basic electronics. My very tattered well-worn and well-used-for-fifty-years Thesaurus,
missing about 25 pages in the middle, sat nearby.

Placing her notebook, replete with key board, in front of her, Debbie put her
cell phone where she could see it to be available in case the school called about an
emergency with her kids. Chelsea, her preteen daughter and Cristian, her son who
was two years younger, had inherited their mother's psychic abilities. These kids
were psychic and open to esoteric things going on around them regardless of where
they were. Appreciating the fact that their school just might have to call her more
frequently because of any repercussions from their being able to see things others
could not, I just asked her point blank if the kids saw spirits at school.

"Of course they do, just like I see them everywhere. I have instructed the kids
to never acknowledge any spirit when I am not with them. Number one, it could be
disrespectful if the spirit does not want to be acknowledged, or if someone in the
room would be uncomfortable knowing that spirit was present. Number two, the
spirit could be evil and it would be difficult for them to tell the difference."

Of course they would have to learn to adjust to their gift. It never dawned on me that even a psychic would have a difficult time starting out as a neophyte with the paranormal. Children were children and still learning everything in general. Mentally chastising myself, I lowered myself onto the fabric desk chair in front of my old PC and straightened the threadbare felt wrist support along the keyboard.

"We really need to modernize you," Debbie wrinkled her nose. She had all the latest in technology and knew how to use it along with all the social networks. "Even your cell phone is a collector's item."

She was right, but I wasn't going there and as usual, when the subject came up, ignored her. "You know my philosophy. If I want it but don't need it, I don't buy it."

"You need it."

"I don't want it." Laughing at our typical banter I moved a box of files and books from my desk to Debbie's work table. "I have enough computer stuff to know what I have to know and to do what I need to do and that's just fine with me."

She shook her head and started to speak. That was my cue to distract her with a nod to the box of books and papers. The ploy was not necessary. When this psychic medium sat down to work with me, the spirits came running—invited or not—and the deck was stacked right next to her with lots of material on the sinking of the Titanic. Evidently, energy poured out of the box and headed right where it needed or wanted to go. Before even mentioning the subject matter or having a chance to tell her anything, I saw that my friend was focused elsewhere.

She immediately smelled peonies then saw a lush well-manicured flower-filled garden. Feeling the thick carpet of grass under her feet, Debbie wished her yard were as nice. Then she noticed the wide hem of a lace skirt brushing over the dense green of the lawn and her eyes followed the cream-colored silk dress up to see an exquisite face under a wide brimmed pink hat layered with big magenta silk flowers.

With that skin of clear porcelain, she is like a Dresden doll, Debbie thought, looking into eyes the color of emeralds. The woman flowed as she walked along with a slightly taller gentleman attired in a black suit. His hair and moustache were as dark as his black jacket. Obviously wealthy, they were discussing a fund raiser for a medical charity.

She told me what she saw.

"You were distracted for only seconds and you witnessed that whole garden scene and you actually smelled the flowers?" I was surprised.

"In a vision, there is no concept of time with the spirits. Fifteen minutes of their time can be milliseconds to the person having the vision. Every spirit comes through in a different manner and not even to every intuitive who is present. Some visions are like bright lights. Some have nice smells like the flowers in this one, but sometimes, there are not so nice odors."

I thought about my close friend who had recently died in a tragic accident. Soon after, I smelled her distinct hand lotion and its redolence hit me hard. Her husband bought it overseas for her and no one else wore it. Missing her dearly, with my grief yet to abate, I knew she was with me in spirit. She had spent time with Debbie to let me know she was at peace. In fact, on one occasion my friend helped her choose flowers for me. Debbie was going to buy me roses and my friend told her I would prefer a spring bouquet, which I absolutely did prefer. When Debbie walked in with a bouquet of tulips and Gerber daisies, I totally lost it in an emotional dichotomy of grief from loss and relief knowing that my friend was content on the Other Side. It was just one of the many things this psychic taught me about spirits reaching out to her so they could interface with the physical world. She was constantly teaching me about the Other Side, like now, explaining why she had the sensory experience in the flash vision of the garden.

"Each spirit has its own technique," she continued. "We, the living, have various sensory experiences. Ten intuitive people can go into the same haunted house and each can have a totally different episode from the others with the same ghost. It is up to the spirit and what it wants to showcase or present to certain people. No one can make the spirit do what a spirit does not want to do, like people on earth.

"Some spirits choose to talk to some psychic mediums over other psychics. If there are three clairvoyants or spiritual intuitives in a room, only one may receive signals from the spirit even though the spirit is in the same room with all three. That's how kinetic energy, the exchange from one to another, works. Only certain spirits share certain energies. Every spirit has its own way of communicating.

"I recently took part in a meditation group that started with a drummer using a repetitive cadence on a Native American kettle drum to relax the group. Among the ten people were a reiki master, psychics, psychic mediums and spiritual teachers. The rest of us were very much aware that the entire room was filled with energy and with those spirits who were happy and comfortable enough to oblige and be a part of the meditation. We all shared what we experienced. One participant picked up only a single spirit, probably because she was new at this process. So, it is a proven fact that each intuitive has individual techniques and results."

Not everyone thought it was proven, but I had evolved from a yes-maybe-there-is-something-going-on person to a true without-a-doubt believer. I thought about her explanation and then had one of my own. Maybe some spirits just did not like some of the living people they had left behind! After that bit of self-comedic relief, I pointed to the box filled with the history of the Titanic and taking a deep breath, just let it out. "Can you communicate with the victims of the sinking of the Titanic ?"

"I probably just did, in that garden."

I knew just then a flash of another vision came through to her. It was quick, but crystal clear.

Humungous almost ridiculous hats swimming in a pool of people.

"You saw something again."

"There were lots of ladies of all ages in long antique dresses under big hats. Really big hats. Really big not-very-pretty-really-unattractive hats from another time period."

The description matched the fashion of 1912, the year the Titanic sank. I could picture the vintage dresses with cinched waists, full skirts and stylized charm, except for those monstrous flowery hats.

"Maybe you really are already into the victims of the Titanic and maybe they would like to let us know what transpired before and after the boat went down— what really happened on board, particularly to them. Scientists can postulate the semantics of why and how she sank and survivors pulled from the icy Atlantic waters or lifeboats have told their varied stories, but only the people who died know how it actually felt to stay on that ship knowing their fate. Continuing to plow through the box, I wondered what to pull out for a first reference.

Looking up at Debbie I asked, "Do you think they are at peace?"

Not everyone is resting peacefully.

Debbie told me a male spirit was in my office and had spoken those words.

"Seriously?" I stopped looking through the Titanic resources.

It was not really a question and not sarcastic, but my tone of voice was slightly unnerved. My skin tone probably dropped a few notches, too. The words precisely echoed those that awoke me that morning. Looking around, I heard nothing, but the office was definitely becoming colder. I felt it. Not frost on the windows, but definitely colder. Then, it stilled.

"Seriously."

"Are we sure we want to do this?" I was getting cold feet metaphorically and maybe just a bit in reality. It really was colder in the room.

"I think you're getting a little squeamish," she noted. "You're the one who wanted the victims to be able to tell their side of the story and I think it is a great idea if they need to share with the physical world."

Setting the thought aside for awhile, we worked assiduously for a few hours on tasks at hand, finishing up business and marketing issues on our recently published first book. Gathering up her purse and electronic stuff, Debbie confirmed she thought it was a positive idea to tell the stories of any of the Titanic victims who chose to accept her invitation, but we would have to postpone the project for a couple of weeks.

"I have several new construction homes to bless plus all my readings."

She reminded me that timing was specific to spirits and we had no problem with starting the book when they were ready and when we were ready. In the past, they seemed to understand when we were not able to write because of things going on in our daily lives and they were dormant until we needed them. I also remembered the ones who just played around with us, messing with the computers and electronic mail between Debbie and me. That concept had been really difficult to accept, but there had been no earthly causes for the inexplicable things that happened. This time, I would be more cognizant and accepting.

Hopefully.

"Just remember to sit and write it all out whenever the spirits come to you and tell me as soon as possible." I had a curious fascination wondering which spirits would come forth, if any.

"I always do and if they have more to say or if we need more information, I want the data at hand to be able to appropriately call them back."

After a good-bye hug, Debbie headed down the stairs and out to her car with me right behind her to lock the door. As silly as it was, I hoped maybe everyone would leave with my psychic friend. I meant everybody. Strange things now happened in my house since we teamed up. Strange things happened even after she left, although she assured me that everyone left with her. Anyone left behind belonged to me. As much as I didn't like to think about that, I was more aware of different energies in my own house because of her. Clicking the lock on the garage door, I set the security alarm.

Like that would keep out a ghost.

Going back upstairs, I wondered if bringing up spirits who died in a disaster was really a good idea. It was probably too late now because of the visions Debbie had already experienced in the office. We already had three spirits who obviously wanted to share with Debbie. Two seemed pretty content strolling through that garden, but the male who said not everyone was at peace made my stomach churn. I wondered again what and who might come forth and I wondered what had we done opening a Pandora's Box called Intentional Spirits, Voices from the Titanic.

I found out two days later.

CHAPTER 3

THE YOUNG MAN
IN BLACK BOOTS

Within forty-eight hours, Debbie called and told me that the Titanic spirits were not going to wait to tell their stories. We had to make time now to start the book. They were all around her. While her children were doing their homework that night after our meeting, she was kneeling over the tub in her bathroom starting to clean it when she experienced a visit from a young man she thought was around the age of twenty. Hearing Debbie tell me what happened to her gave me goose bumps on goose bumps:

The bottom of the bathtub blurred and she realized it was filling with water. Knowing the drain was not plugged, she watched as the water level rose higher and higher. Nearly a foot deep, the surface changed to a smooth wooden floor. Still kneeling, she saw that her tub was completely gone and she was scrubbing what had become the wooden planks of a wide deck. Shiny black high boots stood in front of her. Laced tightly to their tops, they met neatly pressed dark navy britches. Her eyes followed the pants up to the ashen face of a young man.

Cold penetrated her bones. Drips from his loose soaked clothes hit her, biting in as harshly as the air that had changed to briny and frigid in the warmth of the bathroom. Above her, an ice blue sky replaced the white ceiling and she knew she was in another place. Her contemporary lavatory was gone and she with it.

She now kneeled on a huge ship—no, an ocean liner she corrected herself—in the middle of the ocean. Dead silence stood between her and the male form. As she stared at him, she realized he had the sunken eyes of someone who had not slept in a hundred years. His flesh held a bluish tinge and his purple lips did not move. Leaning from her knees onto the back of her calves, she looked around. A restless crowd of people milled on the deck surrounding her in a cacophony of voices speaking to each other, but not to her. They did not realize that she was there.

Skirt hems brushed across the top of her thighs. She looked up at the aloof faces under huge hats of the women in Edwardian dress. Obviously, they were high society and their snobbery came through as clear as a bell. The tragic young man alone, who was evidently not of their social station, was showing her a memory from his time on earth. Only he was sharing these moments from long ago, as was the way of spirits.

We both were silent for a moment. This episode was not an intentional calling of a spirit, but it was exciting for both of us, a confirmation of sorts. I asked Debbie if the whole thing startled her.

"It took me a great deal of time to calm down after this vision. Usually, I just slide into it like gelatin out of a bowl. This time, I was totally unprepared and during the visitation, I was actually nervous. I remember seeing the sky and taking deep breaths. I knew what was happening right away, but it came to me in an offering and I am more comfortable when I send out the invitation in meditation."

Debbie paused and took a deep breath before continuing. "Of course, I welcomed him, but just wasn't ready for any spirit. It was difficult for me not having solid footing, demanding for someone like me who is always in control of the moment. We were under his terms, not mine. I had to be on guard and alert to constantly realize where I was and what I was seeing. The unexpected could hit me, metaphorically or physically, on an ocean liner in the middle of the ocean. I have never even been on a ship before. I was relieved when I came back from the Other Side to my safety net, my home roof over my head, where I feel the safest."

Her remarks downright scared me. I could not begin to imagine how she felt and she was exposed and vulnerable to any evil unless she first wrapped herself in her protective bubble as she always put it. I wondered what we had started.

"How are you feeling about this project?"

"I soon trusted the young man and felt safe with him, but feared he would show me the ship sinking and passengers drowning. Then, I realized that the time of day seemed late morning. Knowing the Titanic sank at night, I was relieved in a way, but because of shifting, spirits moving quickly into a different place or time without warning, he could have brought me into later hours and the unexpected was very disconcerting for me. Once I knew I was back and safe and that this spirit trusted me and wanted to tell his story, my second thought was a need to establish boundaries with him. In this short time with him, we earned a kinship that I want to keep. I knew I could handle it on my end. Someone once said I was like a chameleon and able to mold or adapt into any situation. That's true, especially with the time frames of different eras that I witness, death in all times past."

I dwelled on this for a moment. She was right. Compared with the customs of today, these Titanic victims come to her with their values from a selective time, in this case a century ago. "How will you handle this young man who seems quite independent and quite frankly, brazen?"

"Well, I know now he intends no harm and I am comfortable with him. I know where he is coming from because of his strong personality. He was taking control. After I establish guidelines with him so he can't just drop in, we will be fine. I will intentionally reach out to him and lay down the law. I won't be taken advantage of by people here in the physical world or those on the Other Side. If someone does not cooperate, I sever ties, but this is not the case here. He is brazen, as you say, but I am, too, and, quite frankly, I find him attractive and appealing. It is almost like flirting. Don't forget, he is very real to me and a very handsome Italian, I think, accent and all. I may be a psychic, but I am also female and human."

At that moment, I wondered if Debbie had seen him when he wasn't wet and scraggly, and well, looking dead. "Have you seen him when he looks good?"

"Yes. I will get into that later."

Well, she wasn't going there with me now so my normal female curiosity would have to wait. We were two women talking about one of us meeting a hunky man. He just happened to be a ghost.

"I see him as a normal person and because I see him that way, I know I will like spending time with him. I admire his confidence in just showing up. He is a leader and for this book, I feel he is the ring leader. There is always a take-charge spirit among any spirits called forth for the same reason, always one in control, usually the strongest in personality and the best communicator."

I wondered why this young man. He must have been the one behind Debbie when she was in my office to tell her not everyone was resting in peace and he had no bones about it, so to speak. Then, he just popped into her bathtub. We had two determined individuals in two very different worlds between Debbie and him. It hit me. He came from a time when men were the stronger sex, at least in public. At least they were portrayed that way. They dominated back then. Debbie was going to mandate her rules with a male from a century ago. Good luck with that. I asked her if she had ever communicated with historically connected spirits and catastrophes.

"No, and I don't know why. Maybe it is because of the possible emotion. I have been fascinated with disasters my whole life. I love history, but it is just so sad. On the other hand, I have come to terms with the Titanic spirits because they want their stories told. That is why we are doing this project. I am actually talking first hand to victims who won't be victims any more after they tell me what happened. Not being able to have a voice in the physical world keeps them victims. We are their voices.

"Some have accepted their fate, I am sure, and some have not. We are going to help them out of that because they will share through me. They say what they want. They show me what they wish. We don't ask for specifics at this point, maybe later if we need it, but right now they just come forth and release whatever. You hear it through me, but I get to witness it first hand. For a psychic medium, it's like a kid in a candy store."

I loved history, too, but I was thinking I would prefer the candy store.

"What is your comfort zone in continuing the book in case more spirits boldly barge in again?"

I knew about Debbie's previous experiences like a bloodied young man who died in a car crash and who had jumped in front of her shopping cart at the grocery store because he wanted her help in letting his parents know he was sorry he had driven while intoxicated. However, this Titanic vision was seriously different. Debbie was taken somewhere. It was a spiritual encounter and I could appreciate her concern and I had my own worries.

"Should we continue with this book telling the stories direct from the spirits of the Titanic?"

"Absolutely and I will be prepared. When he came to me, I was totally distracted getting ready for an appointment for a client reading. At that time, I had opened my psychic door preparing for someone else and he took the opportunity. There's no going back now anyway."

Little did we know.

CHAPTER 4

THE YOUNG MAN IN BLACK BOOTS IS ITALIAN

D ebbie called me early the next morning. Chelsea, who was developing her own psychic medium ability, had an uninvited visitor from the Other Side while getting ready for bed. She loved to use her mother's larger bathroom and was in there the night before preparing to brush her teeth when all of a sudden, her bare toes felt wet. The floor was soaked. Drips of water came down from the ceiling and landed into a quickly growing puddle on the light brown linoleum. She stared into the surface of the liquid on the floor and saw the reflection of a man who stared right back at her.

Looking up, she saw him leaning against the wall near the window. Arms crossed and standing on one black-booted leg with the other knee bent back and foot resting comfortably against the painted wall, he shook his head as she kneeled down to touch the water at her feet. Shocked, she felt it and could not believe how much the floor had flooded. It was still gushing down the door frame as if coming from a broken pipe.

Frightened, Chelsea had squeezed her eyelids tightly closed. When she opened them, the man was gone and so was the water. She felt the area where the puddle had been. It was dry. Toothbrush forgotten, she ran screaming for her mother throwing herself into Debbie's arms to sob out what had happened. When they went back into the bathroom, it was now completely devoid of any vestiges of the vision, but Debbie had no doubt about this man that visited her daughter. She knew for sure that at least this one spirit, the handsome Italian man, was trying to contact her through Chelsea. She knew he was the same person who had visited her that night while she was cleaning her bathtub and she knew she had to comfort her children who were just beginning to understand their gift. Her lessons about the Other Side had been constant as the kids were growing up, based on what they could assimilate, but now she would really begin to teach.

She always listened intently to the kids for every detail regardless how seemingly insignificant, trying to discern what they witnessed. Chelsea thought she had done something wrong because the man had shaken his head as if chastising her, but actually, he was not. Debbie was not sure why he had signaled her daughter not to touch the water, but she always tried to pull it all together and analyze the visions her kids experienced. She, herself, questioned why he shook his head. The young girl was not frightened of the man, only of the excessive water because Chelsea thought she let the sink overflow while she was brushing her teeth. Her mother confirmed it was a vision, that she had done nothing wrong, thanked her for telling her and asked her to let her know in the future if she experienced another. Debbie knew it would happen again.

Chelsea did indeed have another incident. Later, she saw water coming from the light fixture on the dining room ceiling. Then, further confirmation of any conception about the Titanic victims wanting their stories told came the next morning at breakfast when Cristian told his mother he had awakened from a bad nightmare at 3:00 a.m. Nothing had been discussed with him about Chelsea's episode, yet he dreamed he was on a small boat with two other people. Three others trying to get into the boat were pulling on him.

Water was going over him and he had to lift up his head over and over to breathe. He felt like someone was trying to kill him, but Debbie assured him they meant no harm. Unlike his sister, he did not know they were spirits that came to him in sleep and did not understand that spirits, particularly those who passed prominently in one way or another, sometime show the living how they died. He could not differentiate between a nightmare and what the spirits were actually doing.

Debbie, protecting her son from having to deal with too much paranormal at his age, told him that it was most likely the memory of one of them showing what happened in the ocean. Grasping each other to stay above water, they inadvertently pulled at him and were not causing deliberate harm. It made sense to her because staff and passengers may have fallen or jumped into the ocean attempting to get into lifeboats. Because of their struggles trying to survive, Cristian felt as though they were pulling him into the water, but in actuality, they were just sharing their memory of drowning. She told her son that the spirits trusted him to be strong enough to share their tragedy. Even if he literally felt their pain, he would hurt only temporarily. This was the reason for his dream.

Meanwhile, as she was relating the dream to me, I closed my eyes and pictured an ocean swelling with brutal icy waves belching up bodies—dead passengers that looked like rag dolls bobbing among screams, cries and wreckage and people trying to pull up others to safety. I felt dizzy thinking of Chelsea and Cristian having a part in this and, worried, asked Debbie how she was feeling about the kids being involved.

"I am not purposely allowing the kids to go through this. I can't protect them from the spirits coming to them, but I can teach them how to guard themselves. It won't go away. They have psychic abilities. Chelsea is older than he is, more advanced in maturity and can understand more about life and death. Cristian doesn't have that maturation yet, proven by his reaction to this experience. Although sad, he knew he was safe after talking to me. I gave him the answers he needed.

"Both kids had very different types of visions about victims, equally startling, but equally explainable. Chelsea saw an apparition appearing in front of her. Cristian had a psychic vision subconsciously in a dream-like state. I know the Titanic spirits are trying to get to me through the kids because I am not concentrating on them, but I want the kids to learn about the Titanic in school, not based on our book.

"That morning, Cristian just kept eating his cereal and banana quietly with his shoulders slumped. He obviously felt beaten, but accepted my explanation that he was a special person to be able to do this and we went on with our day because the whole paranormal thing is a typical occurrence in our house. Some people talk about football. We talk about ghosts. Let's get going on this book. I had no idea things would be happening so fast."

We hung up and I was left with deep ponderous thoughts. I felt relieved to hear that the victims were starting to freely tell their stories. To date, we had at least this one particular young man who had shown up three times, the five spirits Cristian saw in the water and the couple in the garden. On the other hand, I was also distraught thinking that even before we had really confirmed our book would be something we could do, Debbie and both of her children were literally knee deep in Titanic spirits. We had yet to work out the semantics on how the book should be presented. Fiction could disrespect them. Presenting facts as the spirits relayed them might upset the living. Maybe no other spirits would come forth. Maybe we would never know the identities of any spirits. However, we needed to help those souls who had visualized to date.

Although she assured me the kids were handling it and I knew Debbie nurtured her kids to the utmost, having children involved in the spirit world upset me. They were ages eleven and nine and did not have the full maturation to absorb this crossing over and they were still growing into it, gently guided by their mother. I judged and trusted she was doing a great job. By the end of our meeting, she promised to start meditating and to do some investigative spiritual work early the next morning.

CHAPTER 5

THE DEBONAIR MAN

Debbie was floating on a street that materialized where a nice looking man was walking. He was familiar and she thought he was perhaps the debonair gentleman from the flash garden vision. She avoided the crowd approaching them and moved out of the way. Into the subconscious meditation away from her physical life, she intentionally went with the flow and movements of the man dressed in immaculate creased black slacks. He smelled of musky pleasant cologne or soap. Smelling popcorn, maybe wafting from one of the windows that were open to the nice weather, she heard different sounds from various types of footwear on the sidewalk and comfortable conversations among people before easing deeper into the vision.

The streets were bustling with pedestrians hurrying around in wool coats and warm hats in spite of what appeared to be an early spring day. Shop keepers were executing their morning rituals while turning around closed signs on doors and windows. Some put wares outside their stores. It would be a typical day for most, but before the end of the day, it would be significant for the man who now scurried through the crowded street to buy his morning newspaper from a small vendor who was selling them. Buzzing with excitement, those around him were talking about the headlines, and he was eager to read the article.

The front page of the paper showcased the black and white photograph of a monstrous ship. It was "humanly unimaginable in magnitude and proportions, weighing tons of weight and having insurmountable glory". Those are the words she heard. The word she saw in the headline was spelled Titanic. The man placed change into the hands of the newspaper vendor and holding the paper tightly in his own hand as if it were a treasure, he struggled to get through the crowd.

Finally, after walking and walking, he made it to a place less congested where a water front park beckoned. Sitting on a wrought iron bench, he realized how explicitly cold his bottom felt on the metal so he used part of the newspaper to sit on. The early hours of day passed quickly and became afternoon. Typical in the early days of spring, the air warmed to a more pleasant temperature from the cool of the morning.

Warmth from the heat from the sun made him feel like summer was approaching and being in love made him happy and even more attractive. In two weeks, he would see the love of his life, the woman he met through acquaintances of his family who were thought of as family. He explained that, because he was a member of high society, his social peers were automatically respected and considered extended family. His father was a wealthy financier and his mother was of prominent English descent like the parents of his beloved who were also English.

"Close enough to be third cousins," some said during afternoon teas, he shared, but he gladly accepted the arrangement. His fiancé was honored to be coming to him and would overcome her fear of living in a new country. He set aside the rest of the paper and watched children ride their bicycles. Not a care in the world, swimming ducks rippled the water, their wakes reflecting the sunlight. His beloved would sail to a new country as easily as those carefree birds and honored, he would be waiting with open heart and arms for her arrival. Preparation for her coming was difficult with regard to making ready the house and he wanted everything completed before she arrived. The wide floorboards needed to be waxed. Fresh paint would be applied with absolute care to the inside high walls of the large brick home. Chosen by his mother, velvet curtains would dress the windows in the downstairs living room and light curtains would do nicely for the second floor fourth bedroom.

Yes. The plans were in order. A new life was coming home to a foreign country. Paperwork to do . . . landscaper needed for the back garden . . . . "It's got be right . . . ."

Murmuring, he jumped up from the bench to head back to the house that would be filled with a family in a few months time. Taking a left turn after the eighth block, he climbed ten stairs to a brownstone building with a heavy door. Inside, he set his hat on a coat rack and with no disrespect, whistled to announce his arrival. The sound echoed loudly through the large house.

A short plump woman appeared, her big bosoms resting on a belly covered with a white apron. She wore no hat. Square black heels under thick ankles brought her height of five feet up another inch. Her double chin, wrinkled face and salt and pepper hair showed she was much older than he. After nimbly helping him off with the black wool coat that had covered his suit, she shook it before hanging it on the rack so it would not muss. As usual, and with familiarity, she greeted him with "Good day, Sir," and looking him in the eyes, she asked if he would like some tea.

Typically, he treated her like an equal but not this time. With unintentional rudeness, he blatantly ignored her and disregarding her question, ran to the wide open stairwell leading to two upper levels. Turning at the first landing, he passed a library and headed toward a specific room. Standing for a moment, he studied the light pouring into the room that was completely devoid of any furniture except for a solitary piece. Bright rays of the sun shined in from the clear glass in the wide bay window highlighting the homemade wooden crib. Gliding his fingers over the dark cherry rails, he felt a sense of awe as well as a sense of satisfaction. His heels clicked on the wooden floor as he neared the window to look out at the glorious city before him. It was a place where his family would have prestige, honor and opportunities for generations to come.

Memories of his beloved swirled in his mind and his body warmed as he thought about her auburn hair and her contagious smile. Closing his eyes, he swore he could smell her lavender scent. A gentle breeze from the open window stirred the shear lacy off-white curtains and they brushed lightly against his cheek. Turning, he walked toward the door to leave the bedroom and then stopped to look back. He realized that the nursery needed something to match the crib.

"Nanny, please write a letter to the woodsman's shop and ask if they can build a wooden horse for my child." Closing his eyes one more time he added, "Also, I think I will have my tea now."

I finished typing what I hoped was a flowing report from the quick notes Debbie jotted down immediately after this vision and any she had taken later with recollection and review. She was so good about capturing every detail she could remember. Making it read smoother and clearer than the quickly written staccato phrases and phonetic spellings seemed like the thing to do. That became our modus operandi, so to speak. Debbie forwarded her impressions to me and I would hope to transpose them without losing any meaning to the interchange between spirit and psychic. After sending the rough draft back to her, we would recant her experience and I would vicariously go through it with her, enhancing it if she remembered more or any discrepancies. We did not want to lose the slightest of thoughts along the way in relating any story of any victim. I had to admit having a computer made this process a lot easier.

Knowing this debonair gentleman, an appropriate moniker for him, was an intrinsic part of the book, I worked on it immediately and carefully. Debbie was so good at narrating her walk on the Other Side that I knew the foibles of this man and felt every nuance of the setting. He seemed to be in a big city and seemed very much in love for a time when marriages were arranged. She said he looked around the age of thirty. Obviously, he wanted to get started on a family right away and he sure was ready with a nursery. I wondered if we missed something about a baby. For the third time, I studied Debbie's words, her notes taken directly during and after her actual vision:

The streets were fumbling with people dressed in wool coats and warm hats despite the early Spring among them. Stores and coffee shops displaying open signs as the day began to amend itself on a day of importance for one, but not too eager for another. He was dressed in black slacks, pressed to notice the perfect crease in front as he scurried through a crowded street to gather the morning paper from a small vendor. Pushing through a crowd of curious folk tuned into gossip, they all talked about one thing.

The front page of a paper showcasing the black and white photo of a monstrous ship. A ship of magnitude proportions that a human can't even imagine with its tone of weight and insurmountable glory. Handing change to the paper man, he struggles to get away from the crowd holding the newspaper in his hand. As if it were a treasure, he walked ten blocks on the busy streets. The crowd lessens as he makes his way to a nearby water front park. Sitting on the rot iron bench, he realizes how cold his bottom is to the metal and takes a page from the newspaper and sits on it to warm himself.

Children riding by on bikes reminding the population Spring and Summer are upon us, gave him a wince of alertness and joy. In two weeks, he would see the love of his life. The one he met through family, or so called friends of the family. His was one of the higher societies that looked upon others in the same category of financial success, as family. His mother, a descent of England, was no short of wealth as her father was rich in the business of financing. As to say the parents of his soon to be beloved, were also a part of the same heritage. "Close enough to be third cousins," some would say during the afternoon tea. But, acceptable was the arrangement. This information didn't matter. Each breath taken with her was an honored one and one that will overcome fear of a new country.

He set aside the paper and watched as the ducks swam across the river with ease without a care in the world. His beloved would sail with ease to the free land as he would wait for her with his arms and heart open for her arrival. Planning her homecoming wouldn't be easy. A house needed to be arranged and paint would adorn the walls of the brickstone home prepared with absolute care in mind. Velvet curtains picked from his mother and a homemade cherry wood crib would be placed in the fourth bedroom just in front of the bay window on the second floor. Yes, plans were being made as a new life was coming home to a foreign country. Paperwork must be done and a landscaper must come and prepare for the garden out back.

"It's got to be right." He murmured as he jumped up to head back to a house that will be filled with family in a few months time. Taking a left turn on block number eight and climbing ten stairs to a heavy doored building, he set his hat on the coat rack and whistles for help. A woman of pudgy sense and nimble fingers gathers his jacket and blesses him "Good Day, Sir" and places his things on the rack gently without a wrinkle. "How about some tea?" she looks straight in his eyes Disregarding every movement he made and blatantly ignoring her words, he runs on the stairwell into the babes room and stood for a moment. Taking in the suns rays as it poured into the room his fingers glided over the cherry wood crib with a feeling of satisfaction and awe. The sound of his heeled shoe hits the wooden floor with ease as he nears the window and looks out to a glorious city before him. One that will offer his family prestige, honor and the ability for generations to come. Memories swirl in his mind of her auburn hair and contagious smile as the curtain brushes lightly on his cheek from the breeze emanating from the window. He walks outside the bedroom door, but with looking back, and realizes he needs a wooden hourse to match the crib. "Nanny, please write a letter to the woodmans shop and ask them to build a wooden horse for my child." He closes his eyes one more time and includes, "Also, I think I'll have my tea now."

Reading these notes taken while, during and after Debbie floated on the Other Side with this man was mind-boggling and fascinating. His turn of the century manner of speaking and her contemporary one melded as he took her through his story. I was attempting to realize exactly what he was relating.

I surmised that he was prepping the nursery because he wanted to start a family immediately. However, the line about a new life coming here could mean his beloved was pregnant and they were already married. Or, not. That was a kicker thought and it came direct from a spirit on the Other Side, a spirit connected with the Titanic, but one who did not sail on the ocean liner.

Hearing his voice through Debbie was an extraordinary experience. Weird, but extraordinary. Often, the sometimes sketchy notes were just a quick reminiscence jotted in a vernacular reflecting the era and location in which the spirit lived, as was the case here. I enjoyed seeing the tone and manner of the contemporary language in its eloquent phrasing, albeit confusing or even choppy or misspelled because the psychic had to keep up with spirits who traveled quickly from place to place, like this debonair man did in traveling through the crowd to the park and then suddenly to his brownstone home.

Quickly shifting from place to place, he did not realize that someone in the physical world would have a difficult time keeping up. Obviously, this man knew what he wanted when he was alive and what he wanted now, showcased from the Other Side. I had a difficult time keeping up with his thoughts just reading them after the vision.

It may not have been easy for him to share after a hundred years and I knew it was not easy for Debbie. Contingent on their personalities, some spirits were more conscientious and would move slowly with Debbie through a vision. As a strong personality, this guy knew what he wanted and asserted direction, probably making it much easier for Debbie. He seemed to have gone with her flow, even allowing for difficult interruptions.

Executing visions was not always easy. External distractions often abounded for her when she went into a meditative state. She had to focus through even if the outside world infiltrated the sounds of a delivery man knocking on the door or a telephone ringing. With diversions, her sight became foggy while trying to concentrate on not being pulled from the vision and thus, she ended up notating what happened after, not during, the actual spiritual insight.

What we were doing was extraordinarily surreal. Most of the time I really didn't think about the semantics of pulling in the spirits, but when I did give it some thought, I automatically accepted it as truth. She said it was like time travel and I had to agree. The psychic journeyed to the past lives of the spirits. I could brook no argument about that and I wondered if spirits happen to be cognizant of what is happening in today's world. They must be rolling around in their graves, if they did indeed absorb any of the current events, let alone watch someone clicking off a text on a smart phone or whatever. My old portable phone rang interrupting that ponderous thought.

Checking the caller id, a modern technical invention of which I did approve, I answered on the first ring with a big hello while tucking the headset around my ears.

"Hello! What's new?" Debbie's greeting was just as bright as usual.

"How did your house blessings go?"

"I have a picture of a bad entity that I captured with my phone."

Seriously. That was certainly interesting.

"Did you get rid of him?"

"I did and I saved it to show you."

I had nothing to match THAT news, so we caught up on our personal lives. Debbie had some new dental work. I confessed to eating three dark chocolate candy bars. With coconut and almonds. Not a good week for a health advocate.

"It was a frustrating week. There's nothing that mollifies like a candy bar. Soothes the spirit, so to speak, but I need to find solace in something besides candy bars or I will look like my Aunt Marguerite."

Hopefully, my aunt who had weighed 300 pounds and who had been dead for over 30 years wasn't listening in. I had to learn to watch that stuff. Unflattering comments about dead people might not be a good idea. Too late. I changed the subject fast.

"You really like this new man spirit, right?"

"I do and I loved it that he is comfortable enough to show me that he had to put the newspaper under his cold bottom on the metal bench by the water."

I laughed. This debonair gentleman was growing on me, too, and becoming real. I started the third degree with Debbie. Sometimes it seemed like I hit her with question after question. In fact, Debbie would joke that she thought she was under that bright light in an interrogation room filled with detectives.

"He was not a passenger aboard the ship?"

"No. He seemed to be waiting for someone to arrive who was on the Titanic."

If that someone had died on the ocean liner, this man was also a victim of the tragedy.

"Who was he? Where was he? Where was his fiancé or wife coming from? Did the headline on the newspaper say more?" They had to be from the pertinent time period because my psychic friend was having Edwardian flashes of appropriate fashion like the long dresses and large hats. It was a time when a woman and her hat were considered a beautiful thing.

Debbie agreed but had no other answers except that she did see the name Titanic on the headlines of the newspaper.

"Did you catch that he was waiting for a 'new life' to come? That could be his beloved starting a new life or a new life starting in her womb. I just wish he had given you more clues and personal information to identify him. We are like detectives, investigating and researching the data from the spirits. I checked on a few things like the popcorn you smelled walking through the city streets with him. Egyptians made popcorn, so it is possible you smelled it."

"I know I smelled it. It was definitely popcorn."

"I am not really doubting you. Really."

"Sometimes I question myself and have to find out facts for confirmation."

"And, then, if you do that, skeptics will say you discerned data from the physical world, not the Other Side."

"It comes only from the Other Side."

"There were bicycles then, too, so it is plausible the spirit could have been watching children riding bikes when he sat at the waterfront on the cold bench."

"I have no doubt. More than just plausible. I trust what the spirits show or tell me."

"The ducks swimming along the waterfront are a no brainer. Ducks were, are and always will be ducks." I had to laugh when Debbie agreed seriously. "What gets me is the address the man showed you. It was so specific when he took you to the home he was preparing for whoever was coming. You walked eight blocks and then climbed ten stairs up to the brick house. You counted the blocks?"

"Yes. I always count in everything I do. If I walk up my stairs, I count. It seems to keep me steady and focused. I count anything, tiles on floors, ceilings, anything. Numbers are important."

"How many ducks were swimming?"

"Four."

I really didn't expect her to know that.

"Have you had any more Titanic visitors pop in?"

"Yes. Another time when I was not meditating I had a quick flash of two waiters in a dining room. I recognized one as our handsome young Italian. He cleans up great, by the way. His black wavy hair was well-styled and combed back. I saw his dark uniform in the light through the windows behind me. He was probably dressed to serve the dinner guests. The other man was younger. He might be Polish. His short hair was light brown and it looked like a home haircut, like someone who has to do it himself because he can't afford professional services. He seemed quite nervous and uncomfortable like he might be almost feeling ill. He was sweating and showed anxiety so I think he was new and learning his responsibilities as a waiter. That was my opinion." Her thoughts were always short informative sentences.

"I am not sure how you move when you are in a vision. Were you standing or floating near him?"

"I was standing in what I think was a dining room. The Italian was about thirty feet away from me and only a couple of inches taller than my five feet and three-quarters inch."

Debbie always had to throw in the three-quarters of an inch.

"He was facing me with heavy wooden doors behind him. The doors had half moon shapes on them. I don't know where they lead. He was polishing the glasses and silverware setting them on white linen covered tables that were arranged at an angle in an interesting diamond formation around square pillars. Square tables around square pillars. There were squares in the ceiling, too. It was beautiful. White with the squares built in. I think today it's called a tray ceiling. Light poured in from the large clear windows so it must have been morning or early afternoon."

"Do you know for sure that the windows were clear? The dining room on the Titanic, at least the formal one, had stained glass, I think. In fact, I believe some panes survived down in the wreckage. We will have to check out any other dining areas. How do you know whose vision it was? Who was sharing?"

"Obviously, the Italian was showing me the vision because he was the one looking right at me and knew I was in the room. Remember that visions come from the memory of spirits. If he remembered clear windows, that's how he would show it. He was more confident in his work and comfortable with me because he had been with Chelsea and me previously. He was not at all subservient. His hands were clasped behind him in a stand of authority, but he was definitely not as arrogant as he had been before with me. I realized that he and I had come to an understanding on how this was going to all work. It was a flash, not a meditative vision while I was walking from the master bath to the bedroom getting ready to bring the kids to the orthodontist. It came fast."

Debbie was so matter-of-fact and accepting with all these paranormal things just happening in her life day or night. When she was on the right track, confirmation came in the form of goose bumps.

I always experienced a quick chill and goose bumps with all this, but was fine with the whole thing—as long as it stayed vicarious for me and I didn't see what Debbie saw. A lot of people might freak out hearing that someone was transported one hundred years back to a dining room on an ocean liner that sank in the cold Atlantic. It didn't even seem weird to me anymore. Actually, I thought, not feeling weird about the weird was probably weirder and weird always went on when I was with Debbie.

Like today.

"The young Italian man Chelsea and I have seen just came in again and I think he has someone with him," Debbie noted over the phone.

"Seriously." That was sort of a quiet panic word for me. "Where are you right now?"

"In my bedroom, as usual. There's no beginning and no end in here for the spirits. They come and go easily. There's a vortex, an entrance and an exit, an accepting place for spiritual beings to come through in here. Knowing you and I were busy, he just stepped out again. He obviously is growing in respect for me and probably you. I believe he bounces back and forth between our houses. I truly believe that."

Seriously again, I thought.

"He told me his name in your office last week. I looked it up. He was young, maybe in his twenties and definitely Italian, a third class passenger who drowned. He would be considered third class maybe, even as a staff member and I think he was, but he acted high class, well dressed with classy posture."

Goose bumps for both of us. This was hitting home. We knew we would check out his name on the ship's roster for confirmation even if we never revealed his name out of regard to his privacy, but now we had one name relating at least one spirit with the disaster. Debbie was not sure about the identity of the companion of our man in black boots when he came into her office, but hopefully, he would return.

"He is a main character and special in that he was the first to come to you in depth after the quick garden scene. We owe it to him to keep him memorable and significant and I think he was, then and now. He was the leader type then and he was chosen to be the leader of this project so there is something there. I am getting a bit anticipatory about this," I admitted. "It has become real. These people were real. They ARE real."

"Welcome to my world. All dead people were and are real. All the Titanic spirits are real to me. It doesn't scare you, right? I am so happy that you can accept all this and relate."

"I am not afraid, not at all, but promise me again being psychic is not contagious."

Sometimes I thought that it was catchy or something. At times when we were meeting, I heard banging on the wall on the lower floor. This happened more than once. Originally, I thought it was a bird hitting the window. I never found marks on the glass or the pile of wounded birds that would have ensued. The cadence of the thumping came in threes, a few minutes apart. Three birds in a row hitting the window seemed pushing it, let alone it happening over and over. I was always all alone in my office working on the book with my PC and with Debbie on the other end of the phone and with whoever was thumping. In fact, this whoever who thumped was thumping right at the moment.

I told her. Her response was always the same.

"Don't worry. It's probably just your passed friends or family. That's what I feel." She would have laughed if she could have seen the expression on my face.

Then she started to cough.

"Are you all right?" I worried.

"For some reason, I had this all morning off and on. I just feel like I am choking on water and I can't breathe and my lungs are filling up. My eyes are watering so much my cheeks are wet."

She fell silent.

"Debbie!"

"I'm fine. Somebody else just came in."

She coughed a few times again as if clearing her lungs.

"A live somebody or an Other Side somebody?"

"Other Side."

When she spoke, I knew she had gone into one of her flash type visions . . . .

> *"He's an engineer with a bit of a belly and he's in his late thirties, I think. He tells me he is an artistic director . . . that's how he puts it . . . . did the placements of the décor somewhere . . . . . is educated . . . . respectful . . . . good manners . . . hair and moustache black . . . pudgy fingers and he appears wealthy because he is well-dressed . . . showing me colors of materials like wood and furniture, stuff used in interior designing . . . . showing how the beams were installed on the ship . . . . will decide where the furniture will go after the beams . . . upset because they want to put the furniture in first . . . . he said no because it was a safety issue . . . worked in a huge office with others of the same occupation . . ."*

"He just left and probably knew we did not have time for him at the moment."

I typed all this information as quickly as I could and just as Debbie related it. It dawned on me that I had witnessed Debbie while she was witnessing a vision. She was paying attention to him, but had me on the phone—conscious and subconscious working in unison. Good grief, I thought. She was multi-tasking in two worlds.

Right off, Debbie noted the term artistic director. Neither of us was familiar with the expression, but she thought he used it because he was so bright and wanted to relate to her exactly what his purpose was with regard to the ship. He knew she might not have understood his actual terminology. We surmised it meant that he was an interior decorator of sorts. Several resources gave no explanation or definition, so we were on our own to figure it out and that sounded good to us. We did not have the answers to everything, but if the spirit used it, he used it in life and we would keep his nomenclature.

At least the choking feeling overcoming Debbie had eased up a bit and that relieved us both. I had concern, but she figured he had caused it. I still did not feel warm and fuzzy until she explained he used it only as confirmation that he drowned, not to hurt or frighten her. He left before we knew anything else. Debbie made a mental note to invite him to return. I made a mental note to remember to say a prayer before we met about the Titanic book or when I worked on it by myself.

I had questions about the debonair man waiting for his beloved, so we continued with where we left off before the artistic engineer came in. Thinking above the ankle dresses were improper at the beginning of the twentieth century, I wondered why the nanny, or whatever she was to him, was wearing a dress that showed her ankles.

"The spirit showed me what he wanted me to see. It was his vision and that's how he saw her and how she was dressed in the memory. Her skirt was mid-calf. That's what he showed me," explained Debbie.

I believed that and continued reading out loud the new material off the computer screen. I stopped, suddenly, creating dead silence.

"Is everything okay?" asked Debbie.

"Well, a small bright orb just capered across my screen."

"Wonderful! I'm thrilled!" She said it with exuberant glee, always pleased to hear anything she considered paranormal and especially if it happened to me. I was starting to witness and relate to activities she lived with twenty-four hours a day, seven days a week. Maybe I was witnessing stuff, maybe not. I spent most of my time and effort trying to relate and when I wasn't, I was rationalizing my denial.

"I'm thinking it's because I clunked my head so hard on a two by four last week. Actually, it looked like a tiny fairy I saw across the monitor. That I can accept."

Debbie laughed.

"I'm thinking it's a spirit. It could be any spirit. Because it was a tiny flash rolling across your screen, it was a child. That's why it moved that way, kind of bouncing. An adult hovers most of the time. The brighter the orb, the more intelligent the spirit."

"I can't believe I am even talking about this." I still thought it was my mild concussion. At least the thumping on the first floor had stopped.

"We have a few different spirits so far. You go send out invitations to some more. I am going to let the logical and cognitive part of my brain take over and try to forget I saw a tiny bobbing ball of light."

And, to remember that pre-meeting prayer, I thought.

CHAPTER 6

THE MOTHER AND DAUGHTER

I completely forgot about seeing a bouncing orb after bonding with the next Titanic victims who visited Debbie. She surmised right away they were mother and daughter because the older woman ruled over the younger one who still had a mind of her own in spite of the dominate parent. Both had head strong personalities, but the mother was definitely in charge and as we learned later, knew more than the daughter thought she knew. Both ladies were educated and articulate with no poor vernacular coming through.

Having notes from a duet of spirits was confusing to me because it seemed as though I was reading multiple visions. I looked at the psychic's primary notes that she sent earlier so I could prepare for our phone meeting. I wanted nothing lost in paraphrasing the language, syntax, thoughts, spellings and expressions that came from another time, a century ago from these words direct from spirits:

> **Running through the house with a long creme colored chiffon dress that was picturesque with lace and what looked like butterflies, flew effortlessly on the wooden floor. "As I tried to pack the things I knew were needed for the voyage, I truly had the faintest idea of what to bring," she explains to me as she exhales a deep breath. "Heels, numerous stockings, wool coats, can't forget grandmother's knitted sweaters and combs for my hair! They were a must!" she claps her hands as she finished the dubious sentence. "Soap would be a necessity," she stops mid-sentence. "I imagined as the thought came to my head . . ." She stops completely as her mother enters the room**

with a hand full of belongings that a new luxury liner should be able to accommodate, but a woman could not be certain.

The large oddly shaped suitcases were filled with items of the early 1900s as the language of the English women filled my head in awe of their presence. The suitcases were on an oversized wooden bed surrounded with homemade pillows, fabric hanging from ten foot ceilings and a maid dropping off a tray of tea on the table next to the double doors that were efficiently closed once the help left the room. The mother helps herself to a cup and offers one to the worried daughter as they examine every piece of jewelry that will be traveling with them. Rubies of red and sapphires as big as nickels set in ivory were paired with a dark silk evening gown and flowery dresses for brunch. "Hmm. You need more colors darling," the mother says with curiosity and handles a light pink chemise gown with a high neckline that hides everything it can except for her chin. "I despise that dress. It's itchy and has the tendency to add ten pounds to me," She walks to the window with her cup of tea in hand and glances out a large trees and land she's grown accustomed to all her life. "Nonsense. It makes you look classy. Acceptable. You will bring it and wear it." The dress was added to the oddly shaped suitcase and sealed tight with a clank of the levers.

Her mother's hair auburn with a hint of gray, was tied loosely in a bun with curls surrounding her oval face. Red lipstick worn on her pearced lips as she explained, "This corset must be worn with this gown and don't forget that perfume your father got you at Holiday!!" This voice was not one to be in a brawl with. I could tell from the sense she was the curator and a woman of fine sequence. She knew inherently how to pack and her ingenuity proved with the folding of the clothes that she had etiquette.

"Each shoe must be wrapped in cloth. If the shoes get wet, they will be ruined and I did not spend five dollars on each pair for you to be outright careless now." The mother says it sternly with a hint of threat in her voice. "Yes, mother" the brunette young beauty answered with tolerance, a tolerance that would have to be put in order from time to time. It was difficult always fancying a mother's word especially when it came to meeting a suitor on this trip. It was made apparent by a simple lunch that followed with tea and lots of letters mailed later, that she would be marrying a young man that would fit perfect in her family's name and business. He was a banker looking forward to a career in a large city that boasted many opportunities for both families if this worked out. He had handled many accounts before, was well educated and suited for a princess as she. He knew his love of music well and could recite most of the Bible by word. He was distinguished and did not lack anything in the looks department, by any means. She describes him as dark haired that was combed perfectly behind his ears with a small cowlick in the front. He shaved daily and smelled of spice and whiskey that would leave an impact in her nose. He stood at five feet ten inches and had a background of riding horses that helped his shoulders and muscle tone stand out amongst other young men. He spoke highly of his mother, which shown much respect he had for women. Books were his forte and much loved reading anything that was of historical value. Money was the object of his affection as it would be for years to come.

The young beauty would meet him in the States as they began to romance one another with long walks along the brick sidewalks. Talks of opening businesses, world travel and most importantly, intimacy and not waiting for the actual day of betrothal, had succoumbed to ecstasy and impatience to feel one another as lovers do. Waiting would not be impossible as they broke the chastity vow as a baby was six months away after they would marry. She glanced at me with a far away look in her eyes as she just shared a memory of importance one of love, secrets, excitement and declaration of what was to come. A mother stands by as her daughter shares this memory with me, but with a disappointing look in her eyes. She touches her shoulders and gives a gentle squeeze to remind her of the love she still has, despite the bad decisions. Both women stand silent as they slowly disappear into a world of unknown to many, a world of drowning, sorrow, an abyss that only they know of. A barrage of cement blocks filled my lungs as breathing becomes scarce and untouchable. My hands begin to shake and I close my eyes unwillingly with the images in my mind of two women who closely resemble one another, but were so different, a life gone but still fully alive with the memories of those who sank with the Titanic.

I did not realize I had been holding my breath. Debbie mentioned that she felt as though she herself drowned during this episode, totally involuntary on her part, not like me at the moment forgetting to breathe as I read. As many times as I reviewed this, over and over, I kept thinking the text was actually a language from the spirits, wordage used a hundred years ago. In the true sense of the word, it was awesome. The spirits came through this psychic medium with information direct from the Other Side delivered mind to mind or verbally or even with just a sense or by a feeling. I was literally in awe and had so many questions and they were the same questions I had about the man who showed Debbie his nursery.

I wanted to know where they were, who they were, and if they were connected with the debonair man and the arranged marriage and so on. Debbie saw the mother and daughter together, but the vision seemed to come from different perspectives from each. At this point, she did not know why the spirit or spirits showed her this scene of actual packing. Obviously, the trip preparation was important to them then and now and obviously, if the young lady and the debonair young man were a couple, there had been a bit of premarital hanky panky.

Debbie was fascinated with the smells, the architecture and the people. She assumed mother and daughter were going together on the Titanic even though the parent wasn't packing, but rather overseeing the preparation. She probably was going, but nothing was confirmed. Debbie trusted that her meditation with her guides, who had never lead her astray through the years of experience with spirits, had continued to keep her on track. She was confident that these two women were involved with the Titanic.

We were scheduled to have a telephone conference so I called my friend who saw dead people. I said that a lot for re-enforcement with a little confirmation of my own. Maybe even survival.

"It seems like all the notes you took came from two separate people," I told her. "I am so confused because there is repetition, yet I think you said all this was experienced in one sitting."

"Again, it is a time in meditation. These two came at my invitation to see me with memories of the corresponding hours of the same day, yet they have different perceptions of what happened. The vision lasted an unusual forty-five minutes. The same scenario brings different twists from different spirits. It is like when I told you about the ten intuitives in the same room receiving different energies and information."

Light dawned on me. "That makes perfect sense with all these notes. Even I can feel the discrepancies in perspectives from mother and daughter now. I guess we both have to kind of feel it out. Let's go on. The story repeats in parts, but I did the next section like it came from the daughter, a daughter who looked so much like her mother:

She was to sail to a strange land and meet an older man she would be marrying because he fit perfectly with her family name and business. She had met this suitor over a simple lunch followed by tea and an exchange of many mailed letters.

He was a distinguished well-educated banker with big accounts who was looking forward to a career in a large city that boasted many opportunities for both families if this all worked out. Money was important to him and it would be for years to come. He studied music and was an avid reader, particularly enjoying historical books and he could recite most of the Bible by heart.

With his dark hair perfectly combed behind his ears and a small cowlick in the front, he was very well-groomed and handsome at five feet ten inches tall. Broad-shouldered, he had a muscular build from years of riding. That equestrian strength made him stand out from other young men. Always clean shaven, he smelled of spice and whiskey, their redolence still with her when she thought of him. He respected women, always speaking highly of his mother.

She, herself, was young and beautiful and she knew he was perfectly suited for her and would treat her like a princess. Their simple lunch had been followed by tea, hours of promenades and a steady written correspondence. They talked of opening businesses, world travel and most importantly, intimacy. When they met in the States they were to continue their relationship, taking long walks along brick sidewalks. However, not waiting for their wedding day, they had impatiently consummated the marriage early as many lovers do. Chastity broken and with a baby due in six months, the proper length of time for a courtship was impossible.

"Wow," I softly breathed out the word after thinking exactly what the text revealed. With respect, I knew for sure they were not planning a long courtship.

"The mother never knew her daughter was pregnant, but maybe she did know.

Not to be indelicate, but where and when did they have 'conditions' as I believe they used to call it. I bet it was in that garden. The way you described the lawn and flowers made me want to lie down on that carpet of grass, alone or not."

"That has not been affirmed and although it makes perfect sense, at this point I don't even know if the two visions are connected. I am sure that being pregnant and unwed at that time was a big no-no."

"It's a big no-no now. You can't have babies unless you are married."

That triggered a laugh from both of us.

We looked at what seemed to be the mother's perspective from my analysis:

Walking primly and properly, the mother watched her daughter racing ahead of her through her home. The butterflies on the long cream-colored lace and chiffon dress bounced as the young adult ran effortlessly over the wooden floors throughout the big house. She was clueless about what she should bring for this voyage and the excitement of the preparation was exhilarating.

"Heels, lots of stockings, wool coats, combs for my hair and—oh—Grandmother's knitted sweaters," she thought aloud.

After carefully wrapping a lavender colored glass vial of perfume, she placed it in a tapestry satchel. Just as she added soap to her list of necessary items, her mother came into the bedroom. Streaked with gray, the red brown of her auburn hair was worn in a loose bun that matched the deep color of her lip rouge. Her arms were full of things that she considered perfect for a trip on the brand new luxury liner. A dress that the daughter did not want to bring for some reason was included.

Her mother spoke in a tone that brooked no argument. "You must wear a corset with this dress and don't forget the perfume that your father got you at holiday. Wrap each shoe in cloth. If they get wet, they will be ruined. I did not spend five dollars on each pair for you to be outright careless."

Framed by brunette hair, the younger woman's face reflected only tolerance. It was often difficult fancying the word of her mother, especially on this trip. Emotionally distancing herself from the older woman, she pondered her fate.

"The mother insisted on a corset with that one dress that the daughter did not want to wear. That fits, so to speak. Actually, maybe the dress didn't fit well anymore," I assumed. "It was probably tight across the bosom and midsection."

"I do know that the mother never smiled once," Debbie said. "Her lips were always pursed as if in disapproval. Maybe she did know. We don't want to assume and we don't want to project. We take the vision as it came. I take any vision as it comes. Even if it is not definitive, it is a quality vision. You and I are human and as humans, alive or dead, we want answers and we want them now. Maybe we will have answers later and maybe not. Again, we do not disrespect the spirits with conjecture."

In spite of the redundancy between the memories of the women, we pulled up more of the paraphrasing from different parts of the vision to see if we could clarify or make some sense from it. We were looking for any missed clue in my words:

Both women packed assorted clothes and essentials into the oddly shaped dark brown leather trunks that were indigenous to the early 1900s. Eventually, the coverlet on the high wooden bed was devoid of everything that had lain around the now jam-packed suitcases.

While her mother rang for tea, the daughter ran her hands over the plump embroidered pillows and linen bed hangings that reached nearly to the ten foot ceiling. She was leaving all this behind. A maid unobtrusively entered with a silver tray and left just as quietly closing the door tightly behind her. The mother looked at the younger woman's worried face and poured tea for both of them. Each of them added small cubes of sugar to their cups.

"A woman can't have too much jewelry," the mother noted as she put a slice of lemon into the strong hot beverage. Sipping their tea, they carefully scrutinized the crimson ruby and pewter necklace and nickel-sized blue sapphire piece set in ivory. Both were laid out on the top of a claw foot round table of dark wood. The stones winked in the morning light that shone through the tall windows as they paired the gems with dark silk evening gowns and afternoon flowery dresses.

"You need more colors, darling," said the mother holding the necklace over a light pink chemise gown with its neckline that would totally cover the wearer right up to the chin.

"Mother, I hate that dress. It itches and it makes me look fat as if I am ten pounds heavier," she said complaining. Carrying her tea cup, she walked to the double glass doors to look out on the land and trees that had been her world since she was born.

"Nonsense," her mother retorted. "It makes you look classy. Acceptable. You will bring it and you will wear it."

With packing skills sharpened by years of travel, she folded it in three sections with the front showing on top and placed it carefully into the cumbersome trunk. Sealing it with a loud clink of the heavy metal lock all the while thinking that the dress WAS going to be worn the first night aboard the ship, she walked over to stand behind her daughter who was still looking out the window. She put a comforting arm around her shoulder to console, but also to confirm that this mother was in charge.

"I think it came from the mother," Debbie noted. "However, both women had similar and different thoughts of that moment and who knows but those memories might have melded. It is so difficult sometimes to make the division with who did or said what when there is a vision with multiple spirits. This one was climactic. A good part of their story was revealed. We have more to learn and I hope it comes through. Her mother told her to wear that dress with a corset and she would look acceptable. The word 'acceptable' is critical in this case."

"I know from history that unwed women were pariahs. What happened after this vision?"

"When it ended, I came alert thinking how interesting and dumbfounded that I could actually do this. I did not know much about what happened after this moment in time, but I felt only overwhelmed with my abilities on situations that particularly move me. I saw the architecture, the lifestyle, the clothing from another time, all first hand. It's such a wonderful thing, something most people can experience only vicariously. I live it."

"It is like time travel."

"It is indeed."

"How did these spirits show up?"

"I had deliberately meditated to bring up an experience asking for specific spirits who were connected with the disaster. I actually took a chance not knowing what or who would materialize. After the vision I sat quietly waiting while the energy of the room shifted and the energy of the spirits in the time frame they showed me completely left my sight.

"I was thinking how incredible it was realizing I had been absorbed by others from the Other Side who had memories, secrets or even the truth of their lives to share before and after their deaths, especially with the sinking of the Titanic. Each time I come out of a vision, I need to calm myself by taking three cleansing breaths and to stretch my arms and shoulders that seem heavy. It feels like waking from anesthesia, like from a deep sleep. I am still floating afterward and often feel queasy like morning sickness. Before I come back fully, I need a moment or more before I can move on to my physical life.

"It varies from seconds to minutes. Sometimes I have anxiety, but usually it happens peacefully like it did after these two women. That's how it should be, not like the bathtub scene where the spirit picked up me and not the other way around. I did have questions and I needed answers about what I had just witnessed. Why was that memory important to them? They could have shown me anything. There was barely a mention of a father, but the mother was wearing a gold band. I wanted to know from where and why they were traveling. I came back and made notes that the mother paid five dollars for shoes. Sometimes I ask the spirit to speak in a manner I can understand, so maybe that was a translation, or maybe the shoes were from New York, but it should have been five pounds if purchased in the United Kingdom. They had definite English accents, but I did not know if they were in England for sure. They could have been anywhere in the world with their British accents."

"And, you were in your office." My spoken words came out with reverence, more of a thought out loud. "How did you continue to feel after the vision?"

"I was shaky, actually. I felt as though I was smothering, but I sensed the warm touch of someone's arm around my shoulders."

Goose bumps blanketed my arms and legs. I knew more was coming.

"During the vision as I stood on the Other Side, the daughter looked at me distantly as if she had just shared a very important memory of love, secrets, excitement and a declaration of what was to come. The mother stood by with a disappointed look in her eyes, but she put her arms around her grown child and with a gentle squeeze reminded her that she still loved her in spite of bad choices that were made and with a reassurance that her daughter and the child would be cared for.

"Both women stood motionless for a moment before they disappeared into an unknown world of drowning, sorrow and the abyss to which they succumbed. I smelled the ocean and felt a gentle breeze touch my skin and that's when I sensed the tender but firm hand on my shoulder. I nodded a thank you to both women, thanked my spirit guides and left the office quietly closing the door behind me."

There was nothing more that the psychic could have done.

Saying our good byes, I put the portable phone on its base to charge and thought back to that vision that ended with the two women who said so much, but not enough. They had run out of time. Spirits stay here for a minute to an hour maximum, depending on how much energy they have. The theory is that they take our power from electronics, battery operated devices, thunder storms and electrical sources, but no one knows for sure. Hopefully, our Titanic spirits would always have what they need to tell their stories.

CHAPTER 7

THE MATURE COUPLE

"What do you mean we can't call them the old couple?" Shocked, I fussed to Debbie over our phone lines. Evidently, Debbie was also shocked. A pair of ghosts had issued a mandate to us.

"I was really caught off guard, too. We want to show them as much respect as possible, like the other spirits, but they just told me they do not want us to use the word 'old' when referring to them."

"Just?"

"Well, evidently, they know we are working and they just joined us."

This gave a whole new meaning to conference calls.

"I thought you said they WERE elderly. Why can't we call them elderly?"

While speaking, I closed my eyes, picturing my friend in that vortex thing in her bedroom with spirits coming in and out.

"I don't mind anyone calling ME old. I AM old. How old WERE they?"

"They did not say and obviously don't want to share that part. They looked older than you."

"What do they look like?"

"She wore a long dark dress pinned with a cameo brooch at the neck. Her long hair was very gray, tied back in a huge neat bun shaped like a cinnamon roll. One intentional curl centered her forehead. No lipstick, but she had been generous with her face powder. Her well-manicured hands were wrinkled with maturity. He had dark slacks and several layers on top with a long coat, vest and jacket. He blew his nose and pocketed the handkerchief. He was gray, too, but neatly shaved, even the hairline. It always had to be perfect. He was robust looking with a round chubby face.

Not handsome, he was still alluring with a disciplined confident expression. When he reached for a cigar, his wife slapped his hand."

As usual, my psychic friend spilled out recollections automatically, but was still keeping counsel not saying just how old they looked, so I dug in and out loud, read her notes jotted right after the vision:

"Barely holding onto me, I knew he was giving up," she says with an honest approach of her husband. "The cold was so bitter and unforgiving. I thought to myself, this is the way the Lord is punishing me for not remembering to do the Rosary every night." She closes the velvet curtain to her cabin suite that overlooked the upper class cabin. Her hands touching the dark wood mantle of the fireplace, the smell of burning embers fill my nose as she continues to explain why they decided to die on the ship . . . .

"It was fate. A lifetime of memories and this trip . . . this trip was going to be the one we'd talk about for years to come." . . . . A smile stayed with her as she presented a history of conversations about the ship and how this will be the one to witness. "We wanted to be a part of it. A part of the glory that everyone kept talking about. We had the means to do it, so we did," she reminds me confidently . . . .

She sits on the leather bound chair that housed a velvet pillow with a slight stain of wine on the tip of the corner. She rubs it with her hand and lets on how her husband had to come and support this Union. In a moment, he stood there with a white button shirt, ironed brutally with starch and a vest of class that adorned a pin on his left breast. His moustache that of a twirl on both ends and a glass of the finest whiskey in his left hand got acquainted with the cigar in his right.

"Put that thing away!" She slaps his hand with disgust . . . . "I wanted to explain how important it was for us to take this trip. It was more of a marketing thing, really." Walking past the small round window, he takes a deep breath of satisfaction as the cigar left his mouth in a heep of smoke. "Now, it's just a memory, I'm afraid." He turns to look at me with gray eyes and a solemn look . . . . "A memory that keeps knocking on my door!" the older woman rises from the leather chair. Directly in my face, but still holding her sense of class, she proceeds to tell me of how disheartening it is to relive the encounter over and over again. Relatives, paintings, stories,

television, historians and all of those who think they know what happened don't have the slightest clue.

"We try to let this ship go with all of its limitations and so called generational deaths. But with it being around all the bloody time, we can't forget about it!" She slams a foot and spins away from me swooping from one side of the room to the next . . . . "It's over. Done. Finished. I'm tired of explaining this again and again. I want to be with my husband, alone, with no intruders and enjoy the rest of the cruise as it should be."

Her head down and words getting more difficult to hear from the softness of her voice, she covers her hands with his and explains she wants to have eternity with him. She doesn't want any more talk of the boat or the ship's demise or how it happened. They stare out of the window and silence fills the room.

"Wow," I breathed out slowly. "That's sure a different perspective. She knows what she wants. Don't refer to her as old and she wants to stay on the Titanic for eternity and not be interrupted by all the intruders who are legitimately studying the wreckage and those who are rich enough to pay to go down to see it. These two accepted the fact that the Titanic was sinking and chose to stay together on the ship and not fight for their lives. What's nice is they also came to you so you could help them with a final request. What did you say or ask them, if anything, after they shared with you?"

"I quickly told them I would not bother them again. This way they can try to have the comfort, peace and reunion that they were entitled to have through the last century. I did manage to thank them for taking the time to show me how hard it has been to pass away from such an event and be haunted with it even after you have gone to the Other Side.

"The wife was doing the communicating and I was picking up what the husband was feeling, but I think he was senescent. In his senility, he was still aware of his surroundings, his wife and even of me while he was sitting in one of their two leather chairs, still waiting for his whiskey and cigar, but in total denial that the ship was lost.

"He chooses to stay in what is his present time and he is holding on to the tragedy. I also saw a look on his face that revealed he never wanted to admit he was wrong. In spite of friends urging them to go, the wife only acquiesced to take the trip. For him to realize that they should not have sailed on the Titanic would be an admission that she was right. It was only a vacation, a cruise, no particular reason for going. They were retired and did not specifically need time away or even another trip.

"They had already traveled the world. He had a great deal of faith in the Titanic and boasted how it was unsinkable. When it did sink, she never threw it in his face that he was wrong, but rather continued to protect his ego, even in death. That's how she wants it. Fearing he will know the truth by influences from the physical world, she wants to be left alone after a final sharing with me to protect him. I am afraid she will live in eternity asking the same request—please do not disturb us."

Bless their hearts, I thought. She's not haunting the ship. It is haunting her, particularly with those who disturb the vestiges of the great and venerable ocean liner in the ocean depths. Choosing to accept the invitation of a psychic medium was a way to let this world know how she felt and it came with the condition of leaving them alone and spreading the word accordingly. She won't be back, probably, and no way can we disrespect to call them old. In a way, I felt badly helping to perpetuate what a spirit wanted to forget. She wanted only to remember the positives of the voyage and the enjoyment they had preparing for it.

This couple spoke eloquently enough without changing any language that came directly from the wife. Their thoughts are pretty lucid and everything the spirits shared was sacred. I wanted to venerate her by not trying to paraphrase any of her words. She told their story in her way.

After talking with Debbie, I did not care how old they were. Obviously, they loved one another in a unique relationship that allowed a wife to fuss at her husband and slap his hand for grabbing a cigar, but also allowed her to revere him by accepting his choices without reservation. Talk about whither thou goest and marriage vows. She wanted to spend eternity with her husband all the while keeping him safe.

"You said he had a lugubrious expression?" I asked Debbie.

"Lugubrious?! He was sad and seemed emotionally down."

"That's exactly what it means."

We agreed that they had no specific correlation to any of the other spirits we had met so far other than having the misfortune of being fellow passengers. We also agreed that they seemed like first class, like the mother and daughter.

Closing my eyes, I pictured them together sitting in matching chairs of leather and wood watching the water rush into their large stateroom. The electric lights of the Titanic were still lit when she went down so they would have seen before they felt what was coming for their end. What a loss of human love in this physical world. How brave they were, how endearing they were and how very definite it was that this couple deserved to rest in peace together for eternity. Hopefully, they could do just that.

So be it, I thought.

CHAPTER 8

THE MOTHER AND SON

Resting in peace in this physical world was not easy for Debbie. On occasion, we had to take breaks because too much of the trials and travails from the Other Side gave her migraines. She taught classes and took additional reading appointments only to earn needed extra money and indeed, the financial resources were necessary because her beloved car died. She was heart broken, but accepting, as was her way.

Car problems were a fact of life with her. The spirits around Debbie and those brought in by clients used not only the energy in her cell phones, electronic equipment and light bulbs, but parts of her vehicle. Anything connected to the battery was up for grabs with the souls who needed the electrical vibration to stick around. Debbie was always replacing batteries or repairing electronics anywhere and everywhere.

Unfortunately, repairs or new batteries were not going to call her Cadillac back from this kind of dead. The car was not the only energy-drained thing. Occupying many extra hours in psychic readings totally depleted her and assiduously working together with me reliving and revisiting the spirits of the Titanic pulled a lot out of her, too. So, we gave it a rest.

All the while, the spirits continued to visit her in brief moments, letting her know they were ready to tell their stories when she was able. Once, a family of three popped up in front of her while she was cleaning around the kitty litter box. With the cat licking their wet legs, they stayed long enough to tell Debbie that their heavy wet clothing was weighing them down. She thought they were lower class but did not know more about them and promised to help if they came back later. The fact that they had stayed together as a family surprised her. Sometimes when she was alone in the bathroom getting ready for the day, a Titanic spirit would pop in and once, when arriving home, a very young man in his late teens, medium tall and slight of build, walked out of her garage in full form in front of her car. Of course, all the light bulbs blew out because he used their electrical energy to materialize. Another time, an additional victim flashed, a handsome male in his thirties wearing a very wet cream colored shirt. His hands were blue and freezing, but his face was not. Some of these victims who materialized made comments; some did not.

We communicated by computers and she would tell me who was waiting in line for her to have time to "see" them. I was absolutely amazed at the number of souls who wanted closure. While she was still extremely ill and bedridden during this time, Bobby came to sit with her. He was her very first ghost with whom she unknowingly played as a toddler until she discovered he was a spirit when she was 4-years-old. He had stayed with her from the Other Side growing up with her and throughout her life. Now, still caretaking her, he reminded her about the migraines from being physically overwhelmed by spirits even when she was young.

Bobby was the first to take her into the Other Side, the first to expose Debbie to the gentleman, an entity that personified evil. In her earlier years, this diabolical demon had led her on a downward spiral. By the time she met me, she had overcome her bad behavior and thwarted that hideous being who tried to stop her from helping those here and those who had passed. Along with her spirit guides (tantamount to guardian angels) whom she ignored during this dark period in her life, she also ignored Bobby who still hung in there with her if only in the background. Residing in her house, he never deserted her and was now growing up—again—with her kids. The idea was neat to me, although difficult to grasp with the concept of spirits being able to change forms whenever they wanted. Even if they had lived longer to become older looking, they could delineate any stage of their previous live on earth. More mind-blowing stuff.

I knew that information from personal experience with her. Debbie told me she sees her 30-year-old uncle as a mature man, but he passed when he was eleven. He can relate to her easier as an adult, so chooses to be one. Once, in my office, a picture of my father when he was forty popped up on the computer screen. Because Debbie and I were close, so were my spirits close to her. He had been with the psychic on several occasions, but I assumed he looked old and ill like he did when he died at the age of eighty. The photo she saw of him at half that age was the first. Although she had never seen any image of my father at any age, she recognized him and told me that he now looked just like he did in that picture. It was one of those many overwhelming moments with Debbie that startled me, yet gave peace knowing my father was happy staying in what was probably the best time of his life.

When we started up our meetings again, it was mid-summer and the weather continued to be perfect. The hiatus gave opportunities for yard work. While still cleaning the wrath of winter from my gardens, I kept looking at the gong wanting it to move and confirm that my farmer friend kept company. It did not, but I knew he was there. The back yard seemed to be a place to feel my spirit guides with me, like Debbie did. She could see hers. One looked like a California surfer and the other, a short Italian man. I had no idea what mine might look like, but many times I had been "saved" from harm by hearing that "little voice" from my gut or wherever. Something or someone was with me. According to Debbie, we all have spirit guides and we should give them our attention. She also told me everyone had strong potential to be intuitive.

At our first session back to work, we assembled paperwork and all notes in my office. Debbie surprised me with the descriptions of the many Titanic spirits who had come to her. She also had a paranormal story about her house.

"I need to tell you about something about a couple who witnessed an incident at my house in our nice quiet neighborhood."

I thought THIS ought to be good. Adventures of Debbie were always something to hear, especially if they happened in her home. I wondered what the neighbors thought and if they knew just what went on in and around her house. She lived in an area that had been developed with all large houses similar in architecture. Each resident had different landscaping and gardens and the varied yards made for an interesting neighborhood. Heck. Debbie made for an interesting neighborhood. Strange things went on in her house—in and out of it—with high paranormal activity a constant. She could not incessantly give attention to the spirits, but had to go about living her life as usual. It was not a rude thing. They just needed to know she had a lot to deal with in her physical world.

"Everyone around here minds their own business for the most part," she noted.

I wasn't quite sure if she meant her visitor or resident or the neighbors.

"I received a call from a couple familiar with our house. The husband saw our garage door open and asked his wife if we were home. She wasn't sure, so they just watched the house. He was not comfortable leaving the door open, but did not want to be presumptuous and close it.

"Then, they saw a glowing colorful light dancing around the top corner bedroom window, like a disco ball. They watched in awe as this mysterious light continued to gleam. After a few minutes, the colors turned to a bright white and seemed to flood the room with that light. Then every bulb went on all through the house, room by room, one by one. The white turned to a purple glow until the lights gradually faded."

"So, how are these people doing at the moment?" I figured they had a for sale sign on their lawn by now. "Do they know you see ghosts?"

"They do. We know each other well and I had to tell them in case something like this happened. The white light is angelic and a positive good thing. It centered in Cristian's room. Purple and white are good colors for spiritual energy."

"I wonder if any of the Titanic spirits were running around in there. I think some might be impatient, needing to tell you what happened."

"Yes. They know I have time now and they are coming. I brought my notes from a mother and son." Debbie read what had come to her and from her right after the scene:

> **The sun shone brightly on such a cool, breezy day as the ladies were forced to hold down their hats while taking a walk on this early spring day. Dark colors worn by most but all in fine silk, wool or taffeta. Very rare would an underdressed civilian be caught walking the promenade not dressed for the occasion . . . . Large ropes sequined the decks rails as lifeboats hung tightly to the iron posts that overlooked the mass waters. They seemed to mirror the rays of the sun with bright orange and red hues of light. Onlookers sat on the wooden benches, discussing politics, last nights dinner of steak with boullion and roasted potatoes, or whether the holy gathering would still be in effect in the morn . . . . He stood in black leather boots, soaked in a puddle existence, with dark pants and a white shirt, loose around the neck. He stared at me with brown eyes and curly hair that stunk of old salt water and a hint of frozen obscure. No words to be said but the glancing of the wood panels that adorned the sighting of the massive boats structure on what seemed like a painted vision of brand new flooring at sea . . . . With a jerk of his head, he turns to another direction of fellows his age, class and loss. They all stood motionless, staring at nothing, but looking at everything . . . . Voices fill my head of help, witty and horror as they all begin to talk at the same time. Walking closer to me, hands outstretched as if asking for help. "I can only help one at a time," I explained because the situation was becoming larger than expected. Two back away and four stayed to hear of my words but had nothing to say themselves . . . . Silence fills the room as**

the deck of the ship reappears and horror follows the lower class men who gifted me with their presence. People running about, some with silverware, lamps and baggage in hand as they run, run to an end or is it a beginning, of the ships disaster . . . . Too many stories to be told, screams all around and honor lies with the rich and ends with the poor. Children masquerade their faces in elders shoulders while some gripped the shoulders of obsolete strangers . . . . Young girls forced on the boat without their parents, while the older panicked with the situation and told to "Shut up! And, sit your arses down as quick as possible!!" No one would hear of the complaints, or dare say anything of the uncomfortability of the small boats, but be thankful for the existing cohabitants, they were reminded . . . . Remembering of his place that night, the young man in black boots races to his quarters, gathered his things of a small leather bag with a few pants, socks with holes in them, the last of his sixpence, pencil and paper and the bible held tight in his left arm, as he ran down the long corridor with friends all shouting where to go. Tripping on anothers footing, he takes a few steps back to help the other and like cavalry, all ran to the top deck in what seemed like hours but was mere minutes to discover the atroscity of panic. He drops his bag but tucks his bible in his pant leg and runs holding a friends hand. Noticing nothing but darkness, he turns and looks at me with concern and fright in his eyes . . . . I tell him it's going to be okay and he proceeds to show the barricade of others. Man kind hurting or saving one another and the lack of resources that made him understand he would not survive to be 18, nor live in New York City as planned, was a destiny not well received. "I love you mother . . ." he said under his breath while looking at the madness surrounding him . . . . Fog coming in and the air proceeding to get colder by the second, he and his friends parted ways. But not before they hugged one another tightly with "God be with you," out of his lips. With his eyes closed, he jumped into the black ocean with several others who decided it would be best, as well. His lungs filled with water as he gave up swimming and hummed a song to help his conscious mind waiver from the terrible death he would encounter . . . .

Accepting he was of his demise, he stands idling by with a grimace look of dissatisfaction and soaked clothes. His story told quickly and effortlessly as he held nothing back but his bible, how much he missed his mother and his friend Charles. He regrets not being able to see the city and knew he should've waited for the next chartered boat. "The Opportunity was too

good to pass up." . . . . He sits on a wooden stool and shares the story of why he was there in the first place. "Six of us were offered a job in an old abandoned mill. We were supposed to clean it up first, then make room for a warehouse for some kind of automobile plant." Smoking a make shift cigarette, he flicks it off to the ground and continues his tale. "Tires, oil, not sure. Something to do with them American cars." . . . . His silence fell into a state of remorse for a moment as a tear fell down his cheek. "I just wanted to come to America to work so my Mum would be proud of me." I reminded him his mother would and is very proud of him. Not a word from his blue lips . . . . As the room darkened, he disappeared slowly into the mist of the ocean while waiving goodbye with his right hand. I noticed he wore a small ring on the pinky finger and the bible was still in the side of his pants like he left it before he jumped off the boat. The smell of the sea fills my office with the stagnant smell of salt water and the feeling of immense loss as he and the other four leave in unison . . . . A woman in a long flowing dress, high to the neck and hair in a bun appeared slowly and surely walked behind who I knew was her son. She turned to me, smiled and with a silent wave, bid adieu.

Reliving this vision definitely stressed the psychic. Calling it up in her memory not to miss anything meant going through the stress of seeing it all again. Sometimes as I read the visions aloud, Debbie closed her eyes and either stayed with me or went with the spirits as I frantically typed notes adding more details to descriptions of landscape or people. Eventually, the answers to all my questions were satisfied including the fact that the mother and son were not together when they went to the Other Side.

We made this meeting short and when she left, my computer and the new data beckoned. Emotions were churning too much to do mundane worldly chores. Laundry could wait. Errands and the mail at the post office could wait. This saga of these spirits could not wait and being sensitive in transposing this story was paramount. Staring at the original material to cross reference with the notes just taken from mother and son brought deep sadness but comfort in the fact they were now reunited after she had born the grief of losing him on the Titanic. This time, I had taken some of the notes direct from a vision.

While we had been in the midst of reviewing this vision in my office, Debbie suddenly heard a voice from the Other Side. The mother had more information to share and started by saying she had problems with her bones. We figured she was plagued by arthritis or osteoporosis, but in spite of her pain, she worked until she was elderly. She walked with a limp, showing Debbie it was her right side.

That data had just come from a voice and image from the Other Side while we were working.

In my office.

I tried to not think about that part as the spirit continued on, telling Debbie she just dealt with the pain and never complained about it while carrying baskets, doing chores and all the work she had to accomplish at a long heavy wooden table in the large kitchen. She prepared a lot of starchy foods like bread and learned how to sit and move with the least pain. She was wearing a long black skirt. Her skin was wrinkled, but healthy and she shared that using pig fat for her skin kept it supple. This information popped out immediately because the mother heard us talking about her healthy skin and needed to interject. The information just poured from Debbie in no particular order. Then, the mother added that she had another son and she is continually looking for him.

Debbie told the mother that the son was not here, meaning with us. Because we were writing about her and the son who drowned from the Titanic disaster, the mother was tuned in and came to the psychic. Obviously, we had no control over the spirits who could hear us.

Good grief. The medium was talking to this ghost and I was the eavesdropper. As Debbie spoke, I typed fast trying to keep up with all this information that happened in seconds before the ghost disappeared. We never knew how long the spirit would be around. After Debbie told her that the second son was not present, the mother left as quickly as she had come.

Luckily, these brief visions didn't take as much out of Debbie as full meditative visions or readings.

Luckily, I did not lose any light bulbs.

We continued trying to confirm things about the vision without conjecture.

Pragmatically, I puzzled over the automobile part realizing that the first cars WERE on the road a hundred years ago. The sinking of the mighty Titanic meant the loss of more than a magnificent ocean liner. All the men, women and children who could have contributed brains and brawn to this country went down with her. This disaster brought an irrefutable poignant loss larger than the insurmountable magnitude of its size.

Debbie had been on the Other Side with some of them. I really was feeling the need to have everyone in this physical world know the comfort this psychic medium could bring to the spirits of the Titanic. She said they all seemed relieved to have had the chance to let someone know what they wanted to say. I wondered how many more would come. Their stories would all be heart-breaking and some might have the "leave us alone" attitude of the mature couple. This mother and son had so much sadness, but she had given a smile to Debbie before she left her, leaving the story behind for the rest of the world, a story for Debbie to relate, words I could grasp and organize:

In spite of the bright early spring sun, the air was cool and the wind brisk, forcing the ladies to hold down their hats as they walked along the promenade in their finest of dark colored silks, woolens and taffeta. This was no place for the underdressed pedestrian, no place for those wearing less than their finest, to be seen along the wharfs where the ships docked to load their passengers. Thick hemp garlands of ropes intertwined with the deck rails on which lifeboats hung tightly to iron posts over the deep ocean water. Rays of the sun reflected off the boats mirroring the light with bright orange and red. Sightseers looked on from wooden benches as they discussed church, politics and last night's dinner of steak with bullion and roasted potatoes.

In dark pants and a white shirt worn loosely around his neck, he stood tall in black leather boots dripping puddles around his feet. His brown eyes stared at me and his curly hair stunk of old salt water, hinting of that obscure frozen depth from which he came. No words were spoken, but glancing around, the ship was like a painting of the massive Titanic with its brand-new unused wooden decks. He jerked his head around to point out a group of young men of his age and class whose faces reflected the same loss as shown in his. As they gifted me with their presence, all five of them stood motionless, staring at nothing, looking at everything.

My head filled with their horror and their voices begging my help as they all began to talk at once heading in my direction with pleading hands outstretched. This vision overwhelmed me and saying I could help only one spirit at a time, two men back away. Four stayed to hear my words, but they said nothing.

Silence and pain from these men of lower class filled the space around me as the deck of the ship reappears. People ran about, some with silverware, lamps and baggage in hand, running and running to an end or maybe a beginning of the disaster with too many stories to tell, too many screams all around. Children buried their heads in the chests of familiar adults or gripped the shoulders of total strangers. Entitled rich had been honored with articles and stories after their demise. Not so with the poor.

Young girls were forced on the lifeboats without their parents and told to shut up and sit down as quickly as possible. The eldest of the group squelched rising panic. Because of the profanity and tone of those who seemed to be in charge telling them they needed to be thankful for being in the small wooden boat, she realized no one cared about their comfort.

Still looking back to share with me the memory of that night, the young man in black boots raced to his quarters to collect his belongings in a small leather bag that would be filled with a few pants, socks with holes in them, the last of his sixpence, a pencil and paper. He tightly tucked his Bible under his left arm and ran down the long corridor listening to friends shouting directions along the way. Tripping over another person, he stepped back to help him before running to the top deck where others had gone ahead. A distance that took minutes seemed to take forever. In that short time, he realized the degree of panic on the ship. Dropping the bag, he tucked the Bible into a pant leg and ran, grabbing the hand of his friend along the way.

Seeing nothing but darkness, he looked at me with concern and fright. I assured him it was going to be okay and he continued, showing me how others were behind a barricade. Realizing that the inhumanity of mankind over-powered his ability, he knew helping anyone was impossible as well as he knew he would not survive to be 18 or to live in New York City as planned. Surrounded by bedlam and now knowing his destiny, he whispered "I love you Mother" under his breath.

The temperature dropped faster and faster as the air filled with mist. He and his friends hugged tightly saying "God be with you" as he closed his eyes, knowing that this was his only recourse. They all jumped down into the black of the ocean. He was humming a familiar melody for distraction as his lungs filled with icy salt water. Giving in, he stopped swimming, succumbing to a terrible death.

Accepting as he was of the fact that he had died, he stood still, clothing soaked, with a disgusted look on his face. He told me all this quickly and effortlessly holding nothing back and speaking freely of his Bible, how much he missed his mother and his friend Charles. He regretted the fact he never was able to see the city, knowing waiting two months for the next chartered boat to New York would have been a smarter choice.

"The opportunity was too good to pass up," he shared as he sat on a wooden stool to tell the rest of his story. "Six of us were offered a job in an old abandoned mill. We were to clean it up first to make room for a warehouse for some kind of automobile plant." He smoked a makeshift cigarette, flicked it to the ground and continued. "Tires, oil, not sure. Something to do with them American cars."

Remorseful, he fell silent for a moment, a tear streaking his cheek. "I just wanted to come to America to work so my Mum would be proud of me."

I told him that his mother was very proud of him, but not a word came from his blue lips. As the room darkened, he disappeared slowly into the mist of the ocean and waved good bye with his right hand. I noticed he wore a small ring on his pinky finger and the Bible was still in the side of his pants where he put it before he jumped off the Titanic. The stagnant briny odor of sea water and the feeling of immense loss filled my office as he and four others left together.

A woman, hair in a bun, wearing a long flowing high collared dress slowly materialized and walked behind the young man. I knew she followed her son and as he had done, she turned to me and said goodbye with a silent wave.

The skin on my chest was cold. I looked down at the front of my dress, wet from tears still streaming down my face. To date, this young man elicited the deepest palpable emotions of all the spirits. He came, crossing over from the Other Side, so someone would know his side of the story first hand, not by reading books or articles, not by seeing documentaries or movies, but by the help of a deeply moved psychic medium who chose and chooses to care season after season.

Now, with me, now in this book born in early spring and growing through summer, we would tell as many stories as possible. We worked as often as our lives would allow. The spirits let Debbie know they were available. Again, sometimes she could take that moment to listen, sometimes she could not.

Sometimes, they just followed her around.

Chapter 9

The Sad German Man

"I have had a visit from such a sweet Titanic spirit." Debbie's voice was filled with pathos. "He is positively endearing and he seems to be everywhere with me. He moves me deeply."

"Where is everywhere?" I asked.

"He has followed me in the parking lot of the grocery store a few times. I see him clearly wearing pants of a heavy material, a homemade wool jacket and a matching cap that he removes when he sees me. Out of respect, he holds it in his chubby hands in front of him all the time he is with me. His head is balding and he probably weighs about 200 pounds, but he is my height. German, I think. He has hazel eyes in a pale face that is weathered with time and hardship. His brown leather shoes are worn and he walks me to the car, watching as I put the groceries in the trunk and shut it. When I return the carriage, he puts on his hat and waves good bye. He looks older than his age and seems depleted, but he is stronger than our young man in the black leather boots."

"When did he first appear to you? Did you invite him?" I asked.

"He just showed up. No spirit shows up unless they know we can appreciate them and he just needed to tell me his story. We can help him with that."

With a click of an internet notebook, she sent me her version of the vision from this spirit:

His hands were rough like a brillo pad with its chapped skin and rips on the knuckles. He tore the sole of an old leather boot and measured another piece to replace it with easily. Carefully, he uses what seems to be a glue or

liquid to seal the bottom and blows on it as a means to help dry it quicker. With his thinning brown hair, tiring eyes and a yawn that showed exhaustion kicking in, he turns to see the clock strike 7. Ending another day at the shop he takes off his apron and grabs his brown wool coat while he pulls the light string off, signaling another day is done.

He walked briskly on the icy street ignoring passersby doing the same thing he was: going home. Hands in his pocket and a cap on his head, protected him from what seemed like days of rain. The white pale face showed honesty, but also one concerned with packing and how will he settle once he gets there. I wonder where his thoughts go as he jumps from one thing to the next like a jack rabbit in this vision. Using a handkerchief to wipe his nose, he comes to a brown small house with tiny square windows and shutters guarding them closed. Three steps down to the door to his apartment, I noticed it was Dark and a bit gloomy inside. A couch, standing lamp, no pictures, cracked walls and a bed that was obviously a folded cart pushed up against the wall to save space in this one room dwelling.

Papers on the small round table covered it completely, leaving no room for even a cup of tea. The kettle that produced hot water for him to drink was also used for him to bathe with. Not a man with many possessions, but one of an intent to go elsewhere with his dream intact in his mind, he shares.

A brown suitcase, not very big I might add, was taken from a make shift shelf and placed on the cot he had recently opened. Packing nothing but a few t-shirts, a vest, couple of caps, socks with holes in them and apples, he snapped the case shut and sat at the crowded table with a dead look in his eyes. He sips his tea and begins to rub his nearly bald head and with it came tears—Tears from a man who felt lost and who he is, or who he was. Alone as a single animal in a cage, he cries with sadness, loneliness and fear of what he'll do if this plan doesn't work out. A nose red after crying and blowing contemplation, he writes a few notes down on the already disorganized paperwork. He heads to the tiny cot, takes his trousers off and folded them neatly on the floor. He sat on the small bed, does the sign of the cross and speaks in Latin tongue. He resigns the words again with the sign and takes the old blanket and places it over his head as if he were protecting himself. I stand in wonderment and watch him rest but knowing it's not peacefully. My heart aches for him and hopes his plan works out for his sake.

I look around the room once more, and notice only one pair of shoes, a half drunken tea cup and soap that reminded me oatmeal resting on the petite sink. I laid my hand on his head before I bid adieu and thanked a man for sharing what it was like for him, before he set out to another place. My heart sank knowing, he didn't find what he was praying for."

Verbatim, in his voice and that of the medium, the words hit home with regard to the hopes and plans of some of the passengers on the Titanic. She thought the same.

"He had taken a chance, praying he would save his life by starting over in a new place, but instead he lost it. How even more than tragic it was," she noted.

Knowing this man was staying with Debbie most of the time, I felt he must have been so lonely in his life and now on the Other Side that he welcomed someone who would finally listen, someone he could spend time with in the only way known to him after his death. Graciously, she welcomed him.

Obviously, he was indigent. Debbie thought he had been poor throughout his entire life, an existence that had been troubled with poverty and maybe more. He died as an unknown and he deserved not only credit for his life, but honor.

"Maybe we should concentrate on the forgotten victims, like this German man," Debbie noted. "They did not receive much recognition as other victims and we can give it to them now."

After a bit of discussion, we decided first come, first serve, because some of the spirits were better known and their names made headlines in the newspapers and other periodicals at the time. As the spirits appeared to Debbie, we would write about them in that order, regardless of their rank in society.

The wealthy, really as tragic as any of the victims, received attention as famous persons who went to heroic deaths. This German man may not have received even a mention anywhere. Alive, he had been alone on earth and he was alone on the Other Side. Perhaps telling his story would assuage his distress in both joyless life and doleful death.

Tentative about spirits being around me, I still wanted to let him know he could visit with me as well as Debbie, but I could not see or communicate with him. For the first time, I envied her gift of being able to help people after they died. Without any doubts, she was giving comfort to these spirits, some of whom had stories that brought me to tears. This man brought pure palpable pain as I wrote of his last days:

His weathered hands tore off the sole of an old leather boot and he bent to measure another piece of leather to replace it. In spite of the ease with which he repaired the footwear, he felt the chapped soreness of his ripped knuckles as he bent to apply a glue to seal the bottom. Blowing on it to dry it more quickly, he turned to see the clock strike seven. Ending another day at the shop, he pulled his apron over his thinning brown hair and with eyes burning with exhaustion, he yawned when he grabbed his brown wool coat. The room darkened as he pulled the light string, signaling another day was done.

Walking briskly on the icy street, ignoring passersby who were also heading home, he put his sore hands in his pockets. As protection from the rain, a cap over an honest face topped his head, now pale with concern about packing and how he would manage to settle at the end of the voyage. In the vision, Debbie wondered where his thoughts were going as he jumped from one thing to the next like an erratic jack rabbit.

Using a cotton handkerchief to wipe his nose, he came to a small brown house with tiny square windows and shutters closed against the elements and intruders. Three steps down to the door to his apartment, Debbie noticed it was dark and gloomy inside. No pictures brightened the cracked walls. A couch, standing lamp and a folded cart pushed up against the wall to serve as a bed filled most of the single room dwelling.

Papers completely covered a small round table, leaving no room for even a cup of tea. A single kettle served him for hot water for the tea and bathing. Sharing with Debbie, she learned he had little for possessions. With the intention of a new start, his dream was to go elsewhere.

Taking down a small brown suitcase from a make shift shelf, he placed it on the cot he had just opened. After filling it with his few t-shirts, a vest, a couple of caps, socks with holes in them and apples, he snapped it shut and sat at the crowded table. With haunted eyes, he sipped his tea and rubbed his nearly bald head. Tears came from this man who was alone like a single caged animal and who was a lost soul in life. He cried because he was sad, lonely and afraid of what might happen if his plan failed.

Blowing his nose, red from the agony of frustration, he wrote more notes on the already disorganized paperwork. Going to the tiny cot, he removed his trousers and folded them neatly on the floor before sitting on the small bed. He made the sign of the cross with his hand and prayed in Latin. After crossing himself again, he lay down placing an old blanket over his head as if for protection. Debbie watched in wonder as he rested, knowing it was not a peaceful sleep. Her heart ached as she hoped his plan would work for him.

She looked around the room again and saw one pair of shoes, a half drunken cup of tea and soap that looked like it was made of oatmeal resting on the tiny single sink.

She laid her hand on his head before saying good bye and thanked him for sharing what it had been like for him before he set out to another place and her heart sank knowing that he had no idea what he was praying for in those moments.

In spite of the fact Debbie had seen him several times she noticed no one else was ever with him. We agreed that this sad German was our latest most endearing spirit. He died without honor, truly alone in both worlds—until he found Debbie.

"If only for this man, I am happy we did this project," I told her.

"Me, too," was her simple reply. "Now, off I go to pick up the kids at summer camp. Talk to you soon."

CHAPTER 10

THE MAN WITH THE SHINY SHOES

D ebbie called sooner than I expected. Within two hours, I was picking up the phone and without any usual salutation, she blurted, "you won't believe this" in an incredulous tone. That wasn't a good sign. Nothing ever surprised or shocked her and if she were in a state of disbelief, I was sure I was going to be.

"I took our big truck to drive to school, parked in a safe location in the crowded parking lot and turned off the ignition to work on my ipad while waiting for the kids to come out. I put on my reading glasses and suddenly, there was a man in there with me."

Well, that was nothing new. Debbie always found spirits hither and thither regardless of where she was.

"He scared the bejeesus out of me."

Well, that was NOT good. Rarely did spirits frighten her.

"Just as he appeared, the air through out the truck became frosty."

"Where was he exactly?" I dared to ask.

"Right there in the front seat with me. My first reaction, after a slight curse under my breath, was who, what and where did he come from. My second reaction was that he could not have been on the Titanic. He sat politely with his legs crossed and his hands folded on his leg and informed me he WAS a soul from the Titanic."

"What did he look like? Why did you think immediately that he was not a passenger?"

Thankfully, I needed exact descriptions to envision spirits she saw.

"He was dark skinned and looked very young. That second thought I had was that I had never heard of any passengers other than Caucasian aboard the ship. He said something strange—that the ship was salacious. That was his word. He must have felt my discomfort with him just showing up uninvited at this inconvenient time when I was about to pick up the kids, so he started reliving his one hundred year old memories, probably to assure me he was connected with the disaster.

"He told me that no matter how shiny his shoes were, it never mattered. I assumed he meant because of his heritage and the way others perceived it. He seemed a bit agitated, but quieted down and became more comfortable. His accent was foreign and I thought it English at first, but it was not. Maybe he spoke French. Well-mannered, he was also very well educated and intelligent, telling me he had only a few close friends. He said he was strict with his wife and two children."

All this information kept spilling out of her and not in a tidy way, but interrupted with thinking pauses.

"I noticed the distinct outline of his beautifully shaped lips and dark tightly curled hair. He was well built, had great posture and he actually reminded me of one of my ancestors . . . . he wore a dark jacket and a white shirt that had a black cloth tie . . . not a bow tie . . . around the collar . . . the tie was held with something that looked like a pin in front of his neck."

The words kept pouring from her, still not in any particular sequence, until she gently quieted for a few minutes. Trying to envision her on the other end of the phone, I asked her where she was at the moment.

"Well, in my office, and he just came in right now and told me it was a class pin from the school he attended."

Seriously.

Again, I wondered if these spirits always listened in to our conversations or if they ever went anywhere else.

"I was picking up Cristian and Chelsea at the time he sat in the truck, so I had to tell him I could see him later in my office."

"Did you?"

"Yes, and I just sent you my notes."

I immediately opened my e-mail and came face to face with the vision:

"I enjoyed whiskey and can tolerate a fine wine, but not always suitable for my tastes." He wants to get comfortable in now what it is to be in her office and wipes the rim of his mustache with his long fingers.

His socks were black and shoes shined to what he reiterated "wasn't enough" no matter what he did. He shares with me that his birth mother

is with him but sits in silence. His educated voice was one of reason and contemplation but coated with guilt at his passing on such astronomical circumstance. "This never should've happened. It's unimaginary. Inconclusive.Insubordinate . . ." he trails off and turns his head to the barking dogs downstairs in her house who are noticeably reacting to the two spirits sitting in the office. He gets up from the desk chair, and takes what appears to be a pen from his pocket lapel. He writes "Je T'aime les enfants and mon filles." The pen goes slowly back to his pocket as he wipes his brows in what looks like perspiration. She allows him time as she can clearly see his distraught is taking over a bit.

She wonders was he distraught with questions? Distraught with grief? "No, distraught with myself." He answered her mindful thoughts quickly with a look of seriousness in his eyes. "Don't you see, I shoud've known. I should've known." He sits back in the chair and the birth mother consoles him without a word by placing two hands on his shoulders. He reacts by placing a hand on hers and they both stare at me looking for answers.

Silence fills the room as he gapes out the window and notices the breeze amongst the trees. "It was so cold. All I wanted to do was get my wife and children on deck." With hesitation, he cautiously continued. "I did just that. Not knowing what I would do next, I bid them adieu and looked my wife in the eye and said that I'd meet up with them as soon as I could." Swallowing, he finishes with "I knew I never would be able to."

We all sat in what seemed like an eternity just looking at the laptop, or maybe it was so he could compress what he's been holding in. He seemed to take more time to adjust writing his story and that's okay. All she has was time this windy afternoon. "I didn't want them to suffer so I beared the brunt of it. In a different way, they suffered and that was never my intent when I left them that dreary night."

The dogs begin to bark again and she realized the mother had left the room and most likely headed downstairs, which caused the dogs to bark. I asked her to come back up and with a stomp of feet on the staircase, she returned.

He takes in what looked like a deep breath and recounts the smell of the dark night. "It didn't smell like an ocean. More like something burning. I remember looking around wondering where the smell was coming from and couldn't place it. A vest was given to me at that moment and I put it on praying for the grace of God." His holds his jacket as if putting on a make believe vest and I watch as his hands shake. "Grace wasn't meant to be." He stood motionless trapped between his world of the ship and my cluttered office resighting what he remembered. "I witnessed the grace of God when the water froze my body one inch at a time taking my vital organs simply because it could." After a brief pause he showcased his hands to me and said, "I held a white mans hand as he closed his eyes first and I mine." I let go of the vest and floated until I could not float any longer.

Reciting a poem, or maybe it's a song, sang in his native tongue finishes off his appointment with me. No mention of his wife, nor his family that he clearly missed but couldn't convey the messages as it was very painful. She would not push, but allow simply what he could provide at this moment. A moment of telling, one of recognition and another of dying gracefully in the dark, black ocean.

He stands confidently and reminds me of his stature with straight shoulders and educated stance, as we bid one another goodbye. "Such a complex way to die" she says aloud with compassion and sensitivity. He signs off saying to her "what a complex way to live." The smile came through as he entered the vortex of the bright light that canvassed the office. She was relieved they made it through a tough session, but was enamored with his smile at the end. It showed his agreeing with the work as well as support for sharing his story. Until we meet again.

Well, that sure was a shock for both of us. We knew different nationalities were aboard, but not different ethnicities.

"I was also surprised that he described the Titanic as being salacious," noted Debbie. "What IS salacious?"

"Well, it means prurient." Seeing the look on Debbie's face I added, "Obscene, decadent, like that basically."

I was not sure that the word salacious fit into a contemporary meaning. Maybe it was because he thought that some passengers, like the very wealthy, were traveling because of their materialistic values or that they thought they could carouse while crossing the Atlantic. The whole idea sure made for a different twist on the Titanic, too, because we had never heard of the ocean liner as being particularly a party ship. Maybe he knew something historians never learned. These ideas satisfied our objective of trying to ascertain what actually happened on that ship, what actually happened to these real people.

"I am hearing right now that he does not want us to elaborate on his heritage."

The clairvoyant was hearing from this man right at the moment. Having a spirit directly involved with our meetings was becoming the norm. While he was there, we thought we might as well ask him what we need to know.

"What do we call him?"

Not having names to assign to the victims was an issue when writing about these spirits. Just as I asked the question, the sound of a crash came through from the other end of the phone line.

Debbie spoke. "You won't believe this."

"Try me." After nearly two years in working with Debbie, I believed anything.

"My ipad just flew off the desk onto the floor. Then, I heard him say that the name we give him is indigenous to his shiny shoes. Indigenous?? He said that."

"I get it. The definition is belonging to or innate to something, so it means he wants us to think of him with relationship to his shiny shoes somehow."

"You mean what we should call him?"

"Evidently."

"So be it. Let's call him The Man with the Shiny Shoes."

Nothing but quiet came from Debbie's end of the phone. I could almost hear her smile as she told me that he approved.

Hoping he would also approve of my version of his story, I smiled, too, and had a better grasp of transposing the original notes to Debbie's recollection:

Getting comfortable in my office, he wiped the rim of his moustache with his long fingers and said, "I enjoyed whiskey and could tolerate a fine wine, but it was not always suitable for my tastes." Wearing black socks and very shiny black shoes, he noted that regardless of how much he shined them, it was not enough to fit into society. He told me that his biological mother was with him at this moment, but she sat in silence. He spoke reasonably, contemplatively and intelligently, but also with a twinge of guilt from dying in the disaster.

"This should never have happened. It is unimaginary, inconclusive, insubordinate . . ." he trailed from rattling his analysis of the sinking of the Titanic and hearing my two dogs barking because of the presence of two spirits in my office, he turned his head. Rising from the desk chair, he took a pen from his pocket lapel and wrote "Je t'aime les enfants and mon filles" before slowly replacing the pen back into his

pocket. He wiped the perspiration from his brow. Because I saw he was overwhelmed and distraught, I allowed him this time.

I wondered if the source of his distress came from unanswered questions or his grief. Picking up on my thoughts, he told me that he was upset with himself and he repeated over and over, "I should have known, I should have known."

As he sat back in the chair, his mother put her hands on his shoulders trying to console him. He placed his hands on hers and they both stared at me looking for answers. The room stayed dead silent as he moved to the window to gape out and he watched the trees in the wind that reminded him of that night. He finally spoke.

"It was so cold. All I wanted to do was get my wife and children on deck." Hesitating, he continued as if with caution. "I did just that, not knowing what I would do next. When I said goodbye, I looked into the eyes of my wife and told her that I would meet up with them as soon as possible." He swallowed hard and finished with, "I knew I would never be able to do so."

We sat in what seemed like an eternity looking at my laptop. Maybe he was trying to gather thoughts he had held for a long time. He seemed more deliberate in the telling of his story and I let him know that was okay because this time on a windy afternoon was his.

"I did not want them to suffer so I bore the brunt of it. In a different way, they did suffer and that was never my intention when I left them that dreary night."

My dogs started to bark again and I realized that his mother had left the room, probably to head downstairs where they were. I asked her to come back up to my office and she did, stomping her feet all the way back up the stairs.

He took a deep breath and recounted the odors of the dark night.

"It did not smell like an ocean, more like something burning. I remember looking around wondering where the smell was coming from and I could not tell. A life vest was given to me at that moment and I put it on praying for the grace of God."

He held his jacket simulating a life vest. His hands shook. "Grace was not meant to be." Standing motionless, he was trapped between his world of the ship and my cluttered office remembering and reliving his moments on the sinking ship.

"I witnessed the grace of God when I froze to death in the frigid water, one organ at a time." He held out his hands to me and said "I clutched the hand of a white man as he closed his eyes first. Then, I closed mine and let go of the vest to float until I could float no more."

He finished his time with me by reciting a poem, maybe a song, in his native tongue. Because it was too painful, he did not mention his wife and children whom he dearly missed. He could not give them a message. I did not push, but simply allowed what he could provide me during the vision—a moment of telling, one of recognition and another of dying gracefully in the dark, black ocean.

Shoulders back, posture straight, he stood with confidence, reminding me he was an intelligent educated man. We said goodbye to one another. I spoke aloud with compassion and sensitivity, noting, ". . . such a complex way to die." He spoke and noted with a smile, "what a complex way to live."

He passed through the vortex of the bright light that illuminated my office. I was relieved that we had made it through a tough session, but was also relieved and pleased with his smile at the end and the support of sharing his story that meant he agreed with the work we were doing. I thought, until we meet again . . . .

More queries came to me. Debbie and I shared thoughts:

Question: Why the French language? Debbie wasn't sure, but, we just figured he must be French or certainly influenced by the language somehow. He obviously wanted us to know he loved his children and wife and he expressed it in the Romance language in spite of the fact he communicated with Debbie in English.

Question: Where was the paper on which he wrote? He had it in his coat pocket with his pen and replaced the note in his pocket, not leaving it behind. Debbie had not experienced a spirit who materialized physical things, just those who moved objects already in the physical world.

Question: Where were his wife and children if not with him? They were not with him with Debbie and, appreciating his privacy, she did not ask. Sometimes we just don't have the answers, according the psychic.

Question: Were both spouses of the same ethnicity? He never said. We will never know.

Question: Did his guilt keep them apart on the Other Side? He died and caused them pain because they lost him. They probably survived in the lifeboat. We don't know that, either.

Question: Why did his mother stomp her feet going up Debbie's staircase? She was mad because Debbie told her she needed to come back into the office so the dogs would not be a distraction while following through with the vision. Obviously, the mother was not accustomed to being told what to do.

Question: Did his staring at the laptop mean he did not like it? Was that why he tossed the ipad on the floor when we could not think of a moniker for him? Debbie thought that the ipad was just handy and he was probably staring at the laptop with interest because it was not familiar to him. He watched Debbie type notes on it during the vision and being very intelligent, was probably fascinated. Then, again, I have had many moments when tossing my computer out the window was a most palatable thought. I started another list of questions that would remain unanswered.

Why did he think the Titanic was salacious? Was there that much hanky panky going on? We will never know for sure. Perhaps the word had a different softer meaning one hundred years ago.

Why was he so distressed because he "should have known" that something would happen and evidently did not. He could have had a gut feeling. We both had heard that many passengers felt that way, sort of precognitive.

What did his class pin look like? Debbie said it was gold color and round with a crest of some sort, almost resembling a cuff link, but she did not know the name of the school.

After trying to figure out the answers, we both decided we were doing what we should not do. Conjecture or assume.

Debbie confirmed: "That's why I document as much as I can as soon as I can so that every bit of information is available. We can't help but wonder, though."

I sure agreed. It was human nature to be curious. Evidently, it was human nature for spirits to be curious, too. I had learned that much. They were always around when we worked. Debbie was still keeping her respect for the spirits by not guessing answers and she continued with her custom of never referring to those on the Other Side just as "spirit" or "soul" but rather as to their station in life, like "the father" or "the child" or "the engineer" or even by their names if she knew them." To her, generically referring to them as souls or spirits and not identifying them was disrespectful. To me, that's why she was so good at what she did. She cared.

We both cared enough about the Man in the Shiny Shoes to honor his wishes, as we did the others. Questions remain unanswered. Even though Debbie had an audience with the actual passengers who passed, she never pried. They offered. She accepted. However, we certainly learned a lot about the Titanic with this man, knowledge that will probably startle some.

CHAPTER 11

THE FAMILY OF FOUR

After that shocker of a spirit, we foolishly assumed no more historical surprises would meet us as Debbie continued to invite any soul who needed to speak. Of course, in the execution of this project, no spirits seemed to need an invitation. They waited in the wings patiently, or, unfortunately, continued to scare the bejeesus out of Debbie. Her term. I loved it.

The next to show up was a ghostly family of four. Our current phone session had Debbie telling me the details of their initial appearance. She used the term "ghostly" that was unusual for her, explaining that they came through in gray color, like the stereotype gossamer image of a ghost.

While diligently sweeping up the ceramic tile in the family room from the vestiges of daily use and tracking in, Debbie looked around the area that was also the venue for her readings. She studied photos lining the walls over the heavy wooden furniture. They reflected various places she had visited and she remembered good times as she smelled the redolence of lavender that wafted through the air from the candles burning on the green colored laminated bar.

Absent-mindedly, she leaned over to scoop up a pile of sand, cursing her gravel driveway as she used the dust pan. Bending she admired her new patent leather shoes purchased from the local bargain store and brushed off dust from their tops. Straightening to head for the waste basket, she was startled by the family of four in front of her.

"What did you do?" I asked.

"I actually yelped out loud. After saying a not-very-nice-word under my breath so their kids could not hear, I took a few deep breaths and kept sweeping. I never swear in front of my kids, so I would never curse in front of the children of spirits. A client was due in ten minutes, which is probably why I saw them so clearly. My psychic door was open in preparation. I told them it was not their turn at the moment because I had to work with another person, but I promised to reach out to all of them soon. The father nodded and they disappeared. Taking a deep breath, I got a grip on myself and finished cleaning up."

"Were you booked solid that night?" I knew Debbie often had several consecutive appointments.

"I had two more appointments and was exhausted, energy drained, before I headed upstairs to get ready for bed. Removing my makeup that hid the puffy shadows under my eyes, I thought they were more like luggage then bags. I took the opportunity to have a little pity party. The intolerance of having no time for me weighed heavy in my chest as I climbed into the empty bed and rolled over to my right side. Sleepy and relaxed, I saw the father of the family of four standing in front of me. Spirits always show up in my bedroom, so, in the back of my mind, I am always expecting someone and having him there was not as shocking as when they all showed up in the family room."

So much for not even having time to sleep alone, I thought, and of course, asked out loud, "What did he look like?"

"Let's go over the notes I took." As usual, her trusty notebook and pen had been handy on the nightstand when she rolled over on her right side that night and saw him standing next to the bed. Again, her memory was as if she were looking back at someone else, but then she also narrated, but even in mixed voice, the memories of the vision came through clearly:

He stood about 5'10" with light brown hair and a mustache that really needed grooming. He tips his hat to me and waited for my cue to begin talking. With all she had, Debbie sat up and leaned against the head board all the while grabbing her handy notebook. She says a small prayer before beginning and felt the energy shift in the room. With an already dark ambiance, how could it get darker? Well, it did. Much darker. With a blue pen and lined paper, she began to hear the man recite the words "Blessed be God the Father" that he said three times and does the sign of the cross in an Italian way to himself and his family standing behind him who followed suit.

He looks to the left of the bedroom and held out his arm as if he were on a game show producing games or prizes for the contestant at hand. I

glimmer at the site as the bedroom wall opened to a scene on the ship. It's magnificent sight of endless galley ways, children laughing and one trying to use what seemed to be chalk to draw a hopscotch tower. His daughter was frightened by the sight and took her mother's hand. She looked of about 11 years old with a brother not too far off of the same age. "Looks are not important in this" he says prophetically with his hand up as in saying, don't put what they look like in the story please. Debbie abides faithfully. But, the reminder of the clothing was okay. Perhaps second class as the attire they adorned were comfortable and confident. The mother looks down at the child and whispers "Shhhh!" with a finger to her lips so the father may continue with the show. The son stood still as if waiting for orders and only looked straight at the wall with no distraction or fear.

A cold breeze takes the bedroom and Debbie realized she'll need another blanket for this particular vision. Pulling up the maroon heavy afghan, the father presented her with a gift. "A gift of knowing" he says with a secretive, almost whispering tone. She stared out at the ship once more and saw the family of four walking on the deck together enjoying the green sea. Mother and son walking close as father and daughter walked two steps behind talking incessantly on the voyage at hand. The father stopped at a door and peered in to a lounge of some sort, but reflects it as a bar. He manages to squeeze time away from his wife, kisses her on the cheek and walks into a room with about 15 men all doing the same thing. Drinking.

The vision changes to the mother washing the kids faces, no scrubbing hard actually, as she prepares them for bed. It was close to 11 o'clock and she wasn't anywhere near to unpacking yet. She knew once she would get the others too sleep, she could fulfill his duties for the day. Tucking them in, a prayer was said among the three of them including being thankful to be a part of the ships journey. With a twinkle in her sleepy eye and kisses on the forehead, she heads to unpacking.

He tiptoed in the room not wanting to wake the family, but the heavy footing and smell of scotch couldn't keep his wife down for long. She huffs and rolls out of bed to help relieve him of the shoes he had on since they boarded. She gathers a small bowl of warm soap and water to scrub his hands, feet and face as she had done with the kids. With his moaning that led to something that sounded like singing, she kisses him on the forehead after hushing him up and emptied the water bowl that was tainted with cigar smoke.

Fast forwarding to show a day, the family ate fruit, played games and seemed to truly enjoy themselves. No fear, no questioning this marvelous trip. Debbie sat in wonder at the happiness one must've felt aboard the ship at the time.

Quickly fading to darkness, Debbie grips her pen as he continued to show her, yelling, packing, not understanding, confusion to what was happening. His wife grabbed what she could and held both children's hands as they ran heel to heel with others from the same floor. People huddled, many crying others just plain solemn, ran, stood or jumped all around them. "Getting them to a boat, that's all I sought out to do. Getting them to a boat . . ." He trailed off as the vision begins to fade. All four starte at Debbie who was lying in a comfortable oversized bed with a warm afghan around her and trembling fingers. "Thank you" the contestant said softly as the family of four never shared their death, but life. A life that was loving and also one that should be unforgettable.

Footsteps are heard heading down the stairs of Debbie's house as she bids adieu to the family of four.

We decided to just discuss the vision rather than a complete rewrite and we continued our conversation after reading what she had jotted down.

"He was about five foot ten inches with light brown hair and a moustache that really needed grooming. He tipped his hat to me and waited for my cue to begin talking. I sat up and leaned against the headboard after grabbing my handy blue-lined notebook and pen. I always remember my small prayer before beginning with any spirit. The energy shifted in the room. Already dark, it became even more of a dense dark."

Goosebumps went up and down my spine. This was one of the moments I was happy not to have Debbie's gift.

"The man started reciting 'Blessed be God the Father' and said it three times. He did the sign of the cross in an Italian way and each of his family behind him did the same."

"What is the Italian way?" As a Methodist, I was clueless.

"They put their index finger and thumb together and then do the sign of the cross as usual with the Father, the Son and the Holy Ghost. Then, they kiss their fingers and send the kiss up as if to God."

That was very interesting. I had seen Italians do that, but not while crossing themselves.

"He looked toward the left of the bedroom and held out his arm like the host does on a game show when they produce games or prizes for the contestants and in a glimmer, the wall opened to a scene aboard the ship. It was magnificent with endless galley ways, children laughing and one trying to use what seemed like chalk to draw a hopscotch tower. The daughter looked frightened and grabbed her mother's hand. She was about eleven years old with a brother about the same age. At that time, the father asked me not to describe them in what he called 'the story' and I assumed was our book. I am not sure why, but we will respect it."

Well, I thought. He is protecting his children on the Other Side for some reason. Hopefully, we would learn why, but we assumed it was because the kids were frightened. Debbie saw them and what they looked like. He trusted her, so she would keep counsel as to their appearance. He said she could talk about their clothing, however.

"They were dressed perhaps like second class passengers, comfortable and confident."

I was not sure what confident meant, but guessed they accepted their second class status.

"The mother looked down at the daughter and shushed her with finger to her lips so that the father could continue with the show that was like me watching a program. The son stood still as if waiting for orders, undistracted, looking only straight at the wall. He was not as afraid as his sister and seemed to understand what his father was doing. A cold breeze came through the room and I pulled up another blanket, my heavy maroon afghan, knowing I would need it. The father, in a secretive, almost whispering tone, said he was giving me the gift of knowing. Sometimes spirits communicate telepathically, like the man in the shiny black boots, but this father was actually speaking.

"I stared at the ship and saw the family walking on the deck together enjoying the green sea. Mother and son walked close as father and daughter walked two steps behind talking incessantly about the voyage. The father stopped at a door and peered into a lounge of some sort. He managed to squeeze time away from his wife, kissed her on the cheek and walked into a bar-like room filled with fifteen drinking men."

Nothing changes, I thought, remembering the twentieth century cruises I had taken. Then, I also remembered how Debbie always counted everything in her vision and had obviously counted the number of men in the Titanic bar.

"Then, the vision changed to the mother washing the faces of the children to prepare them for bed. They fussed because she was scrubbing so hard. It was an hour from midnight and she was not close to being finished with the unpacking. Once she had everyone in bed, she could do the rest of the chores for the day, including what might be considered his duties, those of her husband. It was expected of her and would make him happy, even though in her mind she felt as though he should help her with the heavy stuff."

Yup, I thought. Nothing has changed.

"They shared a prayer among the three of them and included their thankfulness in being a part of this journey. Eyes tired, the mother still had a twinkle in her eye reflecting her contentment even though she had to do everything as she headed back into another section of their berth to unpack.

"The husband returned and tiptoed into the room so he would not wake the family, but he was noisy walking and he reeked of scotch, waking the wife who huffed while rolling out of bed to help him take off the heavy boots he had worn since they boarded. Gathering a small bowl of warm soap and water, she cleaned his hands, feet and face as she had done with the kids. With his moaning that sounded like singing, she kissed him on the forehead after hushing him so he would not wake them. She emptied the water bowl that actually smelled, tainted with cigar smoke from his skin."

Well, THAT's changed, I thought. Not many modern wives would help their husbands that way.

"The show fast forwarded to another day. The family was eating fruit, playing games and enjoying themselves with no fear or questions about this marvelous trip. I felt their happiness."

I could imagine their contentment, also. Crossing the Atlantic on an ocean liner must have been an impressive adventure. It still was.

"Everything turned dark then. I was gripping my pen as he continued to show me the yelling, packing and confusion at what was happening. His wife grabbed what she could and held the hands of both children as they ran heel to toe with others on the same floor. People looked grim while huddling, crying, running, jumping around or standing. The father was crying out, 'Get them to a boat, that's all I sought to do. Getting them to a boat . . .' and he trailed off as the vision faded."

After several spirits, I was not at all immune to the horror experienced by any of them. I typed, eyes closed as I listened, hoping this one had a good resolution.

"All four stared at me. I lay in my oversized bed, covered and comfortable in my big blankets and my fingers were trembling. I thanked them softly for sharing not the specific details of their death, but rather how their days were spent before they passed, a life that was loving and unforgettable. I said goodbye and heard their footsteps heading down the stairs."

"Did they die on the Titanic or later?" Knowing it was a hundred years ago, I figured the question was not too far-fetched. One of our first spirits connected with the Titanic was not even a passenger.

"I understood they never made it to a life boat, but they did not drown together as a family. The mother was with the children, but the father had walked away once he thought they would make it to a lifeboat. He did not know the difference until they were all in spirit."

They wanted us to focus on how they lived, not how they died. We thought it a wonderful concept and a powerful lesson.

Again, we left them to just be.

CHAPTER 12

CHILDREN OF THE TITANIC

S ummer had become autumn, but not late enough into the season to bring on that golden glow in a morning sun that comes from changing leaves. I wondered if there would be other families, other children, until Debbie called me one early fall night and told me of a day of "happenings" like she was accustomed to experiencing. I, on the other hand, would never be used to hearing of the incidences, especially when she was with Chelsea and Cristian. For me, one should not be a psychic medium until one was grown up.

"We were in the middle of a bad thunder and lightening storm. The rain was torrential on the windshield and I could not see a foot in front of me," she began. "I had the kids in the big truck and drove slowly and carefully. Chelsea was concerned and asked me to go even slower even though we were all exhausted thinking of our warm beds waiting for us. After tuning into country music on the radio, we were all humming along for awhile until the driving became really dangerous. It became even more pitch black, but we were almost home. I knew it was an indication of changing energy, but I did not know where it was going to come from."

Debbie continued with her story saying that she tried to take their minds off the harrowing drive by talking about school and their activities. As they passed the 300-year-old cemetery near her home, she figured that because of the storm, the spirits in there were causing the dark energy she noticed. Heavy rain and winds just churned up the spirits and they are able to materialize easier because of the electrical currents. As her headlights illuminated the venerable headstones, they also shined on an old man dressed in a soldier's coat and pants with a dark hat. He stared as they drove past.

"I promised him I would visit him on another day when it was sunny. I had to get home or I would be washed away."

With everything she had to do each day, offering to return to see him was quite noble.

"When we arrived at our driveway, we all felt incredible relief at being home safe and sound. Because the truck does not fit in our garage, I was slowing to a stop just as close to the garage as I could go so we would not get soaked. Unbuckling our seat belts as the doors went up and the auto lights went on, we heard loud laughter and voices coming from my side of the vehicle and saw a red ball tumbling down the slight hill on the side of the house. I slammed on the brakes so I would not hit one of the seven kids in ghostly form running down toward the truck. They were all dressed in their early 1900s finest and they disappeared before they ran into the truck. At that point, Chelsea jumped up asking 'What was that!?'"

Debbie said she hesitated and then just told her that they were the children from the Titanic and joked around saying how silly they were. There was no need to worry and things were okay. Accustomed to the paranormal activities frequently around them, and because their mother made light of the apparitions, Chelsea took it in stride and with her brother, hopped out of the truck to run into the dry safety of the garage.

"I sat for just a moment realizing how the Titanic children looked as if they were having so much fun, laughing, running and chasing a ball. There were seven kids who had so much energy to deal with and I was grateful they disappeared. Weary from my day and a bit grumpy, I followed my own kids into the house."

Showers, snacks, prayers and bedtime came early that night. They were all deeply asleep an hour earlier than usual. Debbie did not know that her rest would be interrupted by two souls waiting in the wings.

She dreamed she was on the beach basking in its glory, reading a good book. She did not know what the book was, but enjoyed its feel as she held it and felt the breeze rustle the pages. Cottages lined the shoreline that ended in a lighthouse. She was alone in the glory of the sound of the waves hitting the beach and the cry of gulls as they circled the sky.

Peace turned to pain. Her back felt discomfort, waking her slowly. Taking a deep breath, she opened her eyes and saw two figures, one tall and one short, on the side of the bed. Half asleep, she tried to get out the words that start with a muffled, "Hmmph" before she managed to politely ask as she sat up, "What? What are you doing here?"

"We are here for you." The young man said it as if Debbie should know. It was 12:03 am. Falling back on the pillows, she pushed her long hair out of her face.

"Not now. I know we have to do this, but can't you see it is late? I have to rest. Tomorrow." She dismissed them and rolled easily to her side while covering her head with the comforter to make a point. They showed up unannounced and she was entitled to ask them to come back later. Her rules.

An eerie song played on the television that she kept on a music station all night, her tactic to help her maintain the behavior of the spirits. They seemed to leave her alone if she had it on, but not this particular night. She heard music from the television that grasped her attention. The song was *Midnight Madness* and as she was squinting to see the title from the brightness of the screen, the room became dark, very dark to black and strangely, even with the television on. She saw a few stars and smelled something indescribable. An icy chill filled the room as the unknown odor of something burning escalated, but she still did not recognize it. She gathered her afghan from the foot of the bed, hugging it for comfort while saying a quick protection prayer.

"I knew then that these two needed me now, sooner not later. Sooner it was and I invited them in today. And, they came. I need you to revisit the e-mail I sent you yesterday. It was a precursor to this visit."

"I will review your e-mail and type in your vision. Call you tomorrow. Love you."

CHAPTER 13

THE YOUNG GIRL

I usually printed out any mails Debbie sent if they concerned a prospective spirit, so I had the recent one handy:

"Hi Bonnie—thank you for my birthday card . . . . the weirdest thing . . . a friend gave me a purple perfume bottle with lavender scent she found in an antique shop . . . . it reminded me of the one the daughter packed in the mother daughter-vision . . . . a confirmation for me.

"I had a girl around the age of nine, wearing a bonnet on her head, from the Titanic last night . . . . She always hated water and knew the ship would go down!!! She lost her Mom in all the mayhem and locked herself in a bathroom . . . The Mom tried to look for her but she was never found. She drowned alone, in a bathroom . . . . So, here we go . . . . more intentional spirits . . ."

That was pretty typical of the mails Debbie would send to me letting me know a spirit had popped in. Usually, the encounters were a portent of the next spirit to show up among all those waiting in line. Because many children drowned on the Titanic, we figured we would be writing about some of them, but the reality of Debbie seeing this child and what we might learn about her death was tough to take. The adult spirits had their trials and travails until Debbie helped them reconcile what they needed to come to terms with. What on earth would she find in the minds of these children? Knowing that dealing with young spirits could be even more grueling for a psychic, I had never queried her in depth about them.

According to Debbie, the girl in the bonnet seemed shy. Gently, the psychic telepathically let her know that she would make time for her soon. I knew Debbie's week was full. She was working on a school fund raiser, doing extra readings and catching up in her office. Therefore, I was surprised when she sent the attachment so soon of her meditation with the young girl who seemed so reticent about talking to her. My body actually jolted when I read that there was a man with the nine-year-old. Debbie's text was typical staccato spilling out the account as she experienced and remembered it, but atypically, it was written in the third person as if she were watching herself:

Debbie says a prayer with confidence and sits down in front of the laptop knowing others have joined the chilly office. Unobtrusively, "Thank you for today" came out as he says standing with a little girl about the age of nine. "No problem" Debbie answers back and begins to feel the warmth of his attention on her shoulders. Feeling a bit of guilt on taking so long to make this conversation happen for them, was on the back of her mind and was relieved that he took it in stride. The young man knew her thoroughly since he was the one from the beginning, middle and coming soon as an end to the project. The black boots were exactly the same as was his dark curly hair. An immense respect shot between the two of them as he squeezed the right shoulders and placed another hand atop the young girls head and helped her take a step forward to being closer to the psychic. He nods his head as if saying "It's okay" and she began to speak.

With a bit of shyness in her voice that also resembled a mouse, she twisted her fingers together and played with the material on her gray colored dress. She often looked down to the floor and very rare picked her head up to look Debbie in the eye. "Thank goodness you're here with her" Debbie says to him as he nods in agreement. It would be tougher to go through this if he wasn't here, she felt strongly. The other time Debbie has seen the child, the young girl never said a word but shared small visions. Now the medium can see why. Her shyness takes over immediately when attention is on her.

"I have siblings around the same age. I've seen them a few times and we often play but mostly I'm alone-with him." She points to the young man standing willingly.

"Okay, so how are you?" Debbie asked. With a pause the young girl begins curling her light brown hair with her fingers and stares out somewhere

without a response. "Mother would get me cold milk before bed. Not warm milk, cold." Silence fills the room and Debbie looks at him with a questionable look not knowing where this is going to go. "You can enjoy milk if you'd like. You know that don't you?" Debbie asked. The nine year old looks up at him and he nods yes with a smile. She leans on him as if she's been doing it for a century and he pats her head. "I'd like to have milk then!" She giggles halfway between the sentence.

Debbie sits back in her chair and realizes this is going to be difficult and knows she has to go about writing this in a different way. As a mother, she knew she'd have to treat her carefully and add a motherly instinct to the childs view. How do you get a child to open up? She asked herself. Reading her mind, he answers without hesitation. "Well, ask her what she's interested in."

Debbie's back begins to really hurt. Pain shooting up and down the spine all the while her left arm begins to feel like pins and needles. She stretches out her back a bit hoping to get rid of the pain and it stays idle. She looks at the two people in her office and knows one of them is responsible for the physical pain but which one? "I hurt my back when I fell on the wall. Trying to get out of the bathroom." . . . with her skinny arms she lifts them up . . . and it went upside down and I hit the wall." She stares out into space as Debbie types feverishly trying to understand what she means. "No one was with me because I was playing hide and seek. I had the best hiding place. No one could find me."

They all sat for a few moments as a warm light opens up to the right of the office. Debbie tries not to interfere afraid she might scare her little one away. "My sister is calling me-LOOK!" She points her finger to the opening as a breeze fills the office. "I must go! Mother has milk for me!!! WAIT!! I'm coming!!! The young girl takes off like a flash and left standing are the handsome young man and Debbie. He smiles something warm and seemed pleased she ran off with the family. The light fades easily as they both understand time is up for now.

"Watch her, will you?" she asked of him. He answers "I always do." The sound of a recycling truck breaks the sweet monotony of the pair as well as the need to grab a sweatshirt for the chill that runs up her spine. "Til then" he scurries off. "Until then" she replied with a smile. Hoping to be sooner rather than later.

Spilling down my cheeks, tears of joy for the 9-year-old and tears of gratitude for the young man who watched over her for a century showed me how much this book affected me. This vision was so touching and I did not realize how much until later that evening when I was watching a favorite criminal forensic investigation program. A 9-year-old girl was shot and the show's producer decided to walk the viewer through the autopsy. I sobbed. Literally, sobbed.

I called Debbie the next morning to discover that she had the same overwhelming emotional reaction. We were both mothers and that maternal instinct kicked in for the medium on the Other Side and for me who experienced it through her. This child still had things to learn, even in the Hereafter.

"All during the vision, I had to be in my mother mode to capture her tendencies, those of a young girl who was acting just like a 9-year-old. I went with her flow so I would not scare her away and my concern for her lasted until she ran off to have that milk from her mother," said Debbie who was not quite sure why the text came out in the manner it did—third person. "I was concerned about continuity with my notes, but just let it go. I loved this vision. I loved the young man touching my shoulder for support and for his touching the shoulder of the young girl to support her."

I was thinking that if we had to experience the story of a child from the Other Side, at least Debbie enabled closure for her. The young girl could have her bedtime milk, could be with her mother. At least, we hoped, she would now have time in eternity with her family. She seemed happy at the end and letting her go was comfortable.

The young man was endearing and to be that kind, he must have been the same in life. He was the spirit who first appeared to the psychic in her bathtub. We thought it significant and to mean that the book might come full circle through him. The vision, already done in third person, was so beautiful in itself I hesitated to do a précis, revision or paraphrase, but the story that came through was indeed a story and I went for it:

> *After a hectic morning and her prayer of protection, the psychic sat at her laptop. She knew she was not alone in her chilly office and heard his voice.*
>
> *"Thank you for today."*
>
> *She looked to see him and a little girl around the age of nine standing next to him. He touched the shoulders of the medium as if to say he had not minded waiting for her to have time with him. Familiar with her and she with him, he had been with her from the beginning, through the middle and now, nearing the end, with his black boots and dark curly hair. Mutual respect was a constant in all this time. He placed his hand on*

the shoulder of the girl as he had done with the psychic to reassure her that it was safe to speak. Head down during most of the encounter, the young girl worries her hands nervously in the material of her gray dress.

"I have siblings around the same age and have seen them a few times and we often play, but mostly I am alone with him," she spoke shyly, her voice squeaky with excitement. She was up and down emotionally, typical of that age, and the medium had a difficult time keeping up with her.

Grateful of the young man's presence that reassured the girl, the medium thanked him for bringing her. He acknowledged her gratitude with a nod. Previously, the girl had allowed quick quiet visions, only flashes, but now, even though self-conscious about being the center of attention, she was willing to tell her story with her friend at her side.

The psychic asked her how she was doing. Hesitating, her fingers now twisted her long light brown hair into curls as she stared at nothing and finally admitted, "Mother would get me cold milk before bed. Not warm milk, cold."

The room was silent. Not knowing where this was going, the psychic looked at the young man as if for guidance and then told the 9-year-old, "You know you can enjoy milk if you would like. You know that don't you?"

The young man looked down into the face of the young girl and smiling, he nodded to confirm. As he patted her head, she leaned against him with the comfort and familiarity of having done it for a hundred years.

Giggling, she announced, "I would like to have milk then!"

The psychic thought she must tread softly as to not frighten the child in eliciting her to open up. The young man read her mind and suggested that she ask the child about her interests. Back pain shot up and down her spine and she wondered which of the two spirits had that physical malady. Staring into space, the young girl immediately spoke.

"I hurt my back when I fell on the wall. Trying to get out of the room . . ." She lifted her skinny arms. ". . . and it went upside down and I hit the wall."

Wondering what this meant, the psychic continued to type as the girl continued to speak.

"No one was with me because I was playing hide and seek. I had the best hiding place. No one could find me."

The three of them sat quietly for a few minutes until a warm light opened up to the right of the office. Fearing she might scare off the little one, the psychic did not react.

"My sister is calling me-LOOK!" The girl pointed to the opening and a breeze filled the office. "I must go. Mother had milk for me!! WAIT!! I am coming!" With that,

she took off in a flash toward her family leaving the young man spirit alone with the medium.

Pleased, he smiled warmly as the light easily faded. They both understood their time was up. The psychic spoke first.

"Watch her, will you?"

"I always do."

The physical world interrupted their moment with the sound of a recycling truck. The psychic grabbed her sweatshirt to ward off the chill settling in her sore spine.

"Til' then," he said.

"Until then," she said smiling, hoping it would be sooner than later.

This nice young man, so kind to a child, was the same who scared Debbie while she was cleaning the bath tub. She said she understood the little girl hung around him because she was alone. He must have been so incredibly thoughtful, unselfish and patient in life and now in death.

"Perhaps because she was by herself, he felt compelled to introduce her to us because she was not with an adult," Debbie explained. "Also, he may have gleaned from me that I am more comfortable interviewing or taking vision in meditation from a child when an adult is present, so he came with her. Working with children can be tricky. I don't give readings to anyone under the age of 18 for that reason."

Knowing how sensitive young people can be, that made perfect sense to me. This young man escorting our 9-year-old was just a perfect thing to experience. It suddenly dawned on me that I said "our" 9-year-old. Both Debbie and I had started saying "we" or "us" with reference to the spirits telling their stories. I was more deeply involved with the spirit world than before or after working with my friend, the psychic medium, but not, of course to her level. I thanked my spirit guides for that. Just being aware was enough for me.

"Debbie, I have an important question," I postured. "Can spirits really drink milk on the Other Side?"

"Yes."

"You mean I can have all the coconut and dark chocolate bars I want?"

"Absolutely."

Well, that and bright light and angels and God. Who could want more from Heaven?

CHAPTER 14

THE YOUNG MAN IN THE
BLACK BOOTS AGAIN

He stood there motionless by the side of Debbie's bed. Without a word being said, each knew what the other was thinking. It was 12:37 A.M. and work needed to be done. Consciously, she awoke feeling his timeless energy and urgency to the project at hand. Wiping the sleep from her eyes, she walks slowly down the staircase to retrieve a cold bottle of water.

He follows her carefully, as to not awaken the family pets. The bright light from the fridge sheds notice to the several choices of flavored water. "White Grape it is," she said aloud. Twisting open the cap, he asks what it tastes like. "Well, it's really cold going down the throat," she explains. "As the water was for me when I died," he answered quickly.

Total silence filled the kitchen as she took a seat on the counter stool. Rubbing her hands on the very tired face, she took a deep breath knowing what he was here for. "Tomorrow, we will write." With that, she pushed the stool back to the counter and headed back up the stairs with him behind her. She climbed back into the warm bed as he stood wary of her exhaustion and bid her good night.

The morning came welcoming everyone in the household with a ray of sunshine. It was much needed and enjoyed after days of heavy rain and wind. After the children and spouse perish to visit with family, Debbie knew this would be a wonderful, but sad day to herself . . . A day of closure, but also an opening . . . . A day of reconciliation, or reckoning . . . . One with spirit, or spirits . . . . A day of not knowing, but knowing . . . .

She carefully loads the laptop that takes over a half hour to boot its memory, due to energy gathering in the organized office. She sits patiently and asks for spirit not to interfere with the laptop and within a minute, the computer begins to log in. "Thank you." She mumbled under her breath. "Tis the life of a Medium." . . . . She stretches her fingers and rubs her arms as if to react to the cold infusion of air surrounding her. A prayer and request has been sent with an answer coming quick as lightning. Words are heard, steps taken in the room and objects shove deeper down into the trash barrel as if someone is pushing them. Debbie peers around and asks for silence for a moment so she could take in what was happening. Excitement, awe and trepidation become one as she closes her eyes to see what there was to see.

The color purple lines the sky and magically turns to blue. Shadows appear one by one as she focuses on sound, as well as sight. Footsteps on the hardened floor wake her senses while smelling the sea air. Happiness all around her as those who seemed lost have found heavenly glory. A woman comes up to her wearing a veil hung delicately over her bun and pats Debbie on the back for a job well done. An immediate response of "Thank you" comes from her lips as the woman prances away in her long dress with a smile. Kids run past the huge deck as the wind picks up from the North. She glances over and sees him with his black boots and dark hair leaning on the rail. Walking over the sound of her present shoes clanking over the wood protectively as she tries not to make a scene to interrupt spirits glorious afternoon. She humbly stands next to him as they both look over the boats edge. Ignoring the sounds around them, what seemed to matter the most was the ocean. It's peek of brightness also surrounded by her shades of darkness. Breathing in the air, Debbie realizes it slowly becomes the night.

Passengers were scarce as the time went swiftly on as if they found shelter from the cold from the many doors that lay course around the ship. His hair blows with the wind as the sound of chaos rings true. He looks at her and says "Be brave," as he took her hands off of her ears to witness the cries and struggles of those that perished. Feeling the ship move beneath her feet, she held onto the rail in this uncomfortable, but needful meditation. He held her hand on the freezing pole and acknowledged what she felt. Terror . . . .

"This is not okay. This is NOT OKAY!" Debbie repeats over and over in her mind. "No, it's not." He answered.

They begin to spin like a top that has no limit but can be controlled. They stop in a dining room as a vision of two girls who seemed to look exactly alike, ran past them without acknowledging either one. "Looking for hope. That's what I remember. Never to be found." He swoops her to the staircase and slides down the banister laughing and jumping off at the very end. "Come with me!" he says with a hand in the airNo way. I'll walk, thank you." Debbie glides instead of walks in his vision and he waits patiently for her to get to the stairs. How can he go from a terrifying moment to one of fun bliss? She asks herself. I guess it's the way he's dealing with it.

He sits against the wall with his elbows on top of the knees staring at the empty room. She walked up to him slowly not knowing what would come next. "There used to be so many of us here. Waiting. Praying. In this very room. He sounded so convincing. With a pointed finger he says, "You could walk right out that door and have the most spectacular view ever." He quiets for a moment and adds "A view of eternity. Ever notice how the ocean line never ends? Eternity." He finishes . . . .

The dark eyes of the young man stare into open space of the vision he carefully chosen for her. A tear runs down his left cheek brazen with cold air. She shivers with sadness, perhaps with a wonder of death being so, well, eternal. "I do notice that. It's eternity, I mean." With an understanding he grabs her hand and whisks her back into the small office space. Sitting in the desk chair. He knelt on the left knee and bowed his head in thanks. He holds one hand of hers as he looked down to the floor and up at her again to assure with defining words "This isn't over. It's only begun." . . . .

She cried knowing the truth in her friends words and knew she had to complete the part of his character in the book, but was secretly excited it wouldn't be over completely as he included "begun". She turns in the chair as she slowly comes out of the eclectic scenes shared and noticed the paragraphs of knowing and reckoning, as well as the one spirit who guided many to what they know of as eternity. A gentle breeze leaves the room and her head fills with bittersweet thankfulness, as she feels the residual energy of the Titanic.

I read this and for some unknown reason, was so downcast. It dawned on me that the book had obviously come full circle to an ending and I did not want to let go of the Titanic spirits. This young Italian never gave a lot of details about himself, but he was so strong in spirit and was the spokesperson for others, the one who organized or persuaded others to come. In the beginning, Debbie called him a ring-leader and said he would be pivotal to the story. He was. I really did not want to let him go and I wrote it again:

The clock read 12:37 a.m. when she saw him standing still next to the bed. They both knew the urgency of their project.

He had time.

She did not.

She needed to wake up and walked slowly and quietly downstairs so she would not wake the pets. Taking a bottle of white grape flavored water from the brightness of the refrigerator, she twisted the cap as he asked what it tasted like and she told him it is very cold going down the throat.

"As the water was for me when I died," he responded immediately.

Total silence filled the kitchen. Sitting on a counter stool, she rubbed her hands over her tired face. Knowing why he was here, she took a deep breath and said, "Tomorrow, we will write." Pushing away from the stool, she felt him follow her back up the stairs. She climbed into her warm bed and he stood there, not knowing why she was so exhausted. He said good night.

The following morning dawned bright with welcomed sun after a spell of dreary rainy days. After her family left to visit relatives, she had the house to herself. She knew it would be a wonderful, but sad day, a day of closure but an opening, a day of reconciliation and reckoning, one of knowing or not knowing, a day with spirit or spirits.

Carefully booting up her laptop, she noticed that took much longer to engage due to the building energy in her newly organized office. Patiently, she asked that spirit not interfere with the computer and within a minute, her request was granted by the laptop logging in. "Such is the life of a medium," she mumbled while stretching her fingers and arms in the cold starting to surround her. She prayed and requested, answered by words and steps heard. Paper crinkled with the sound of it being pushed down forcefully into the trash bucket and she looked around asking spirit for a silent moment to regroup. Excitement, awe and trepidation melded as she closed her eyes.

She saw purple color lining a sky that magically turned blue. One by one, shadows appeared and she focused on sound, sight and the smell of the sea. Footsteps on her hardwood floor heightened her awareness of the happiness surrounding her from those who seemed lost but who have found heavenly glory. A woman with a delicate veil over her hair patted her on the back in congratulations of a job well done. Thanking her, the psychic watched the smiling woman bounce away in her long dress. Kids ran along the huge deck and the wind from the North started to blow harder.

Glancing over, she saw him with his black boots and dark hair leaning against the railing. She walked over, trying not to make noise with her shoes in order not to disrupt the glorious afternoon enjoyed by the spirits. Amazed at experiencing all this, she stood humble next to him and they both looked over the edge of the ship. The ocean was what mattered, not the sounds around them. It peeked bright, framed by her shades of darkness. Breathing in the air, she realized she was now in the cool of the night. The decks were not as congested. Passengers had sought shelter in their cabins.

His hair blew with the wind. Chaos began and he told her to be brave, taking her hands from her ears so she could witness the cries and struggles of those that perished. Feeling the ship move beneath her feet, she held onto the rail in this uncomfortable, but necessary, meditation. His hand was over hers on the railing to acknowledge what she felt. Losing control of herself in the vision, she cried, repeating it over and over in her mind, "This is not okay, this is NOT OKAY!"

"No, it's not," he agreed. They started to spin like a top in a circle until it stopped in a dining room. Twin girls ran past them and did not acknowledge the couple. "Looking for hope," he said. "That's what I remember. Never to be found."

He transported her to the staircase and slid down the banister laughing and jumping off at the very end, waving his hand in the air and saying, "Come with me!" The medium declined, gliding instead of walking in his vision and he waited patiently for her to reach the stairs. Wondering how he could go from terror to bliss, she decided it is his way of dealing. Sitting against the wall with his elbows on top of his knees, he stared into the empty room. She walked up to him slowly, not sure of what was next.

"There used to be so many of us here. Waiting. Praying. In this very room . . ." He sounded so convincing. Pointing his finger to a door he said, "You could walk right out that door and have the most spectacular view ever." He quieted for a moment and added, "A view of eternity. Ever notice how the ocean line never ends? Eternity." His dark eyes stared into the open space of the vision carefully chosen for her and a tear runs down his left cheek, brittle from the frigid air.

She shivered in sadness and with a wonder of death being so eternal. "I do notice that. Its eternity, I mean."

Understanding, he grabbed her hand and whisked her back into her small office and her chair. He knelt, head bowed, giving thanks. Still holding her hand, he looked down to the floor and back up at her to assert, "This isn't over. It's only begun."

She cried, knowing the truth in the words of this friend and also knowing she had to finish his part in the book. Secretly, she was excited it would not be over completely because of his promise.

She turned in the chair slowly coming out of the eclectic scenes shared with her and saw her notes. He wanted to bring the reader of the book to terms in a realization and a reckoning of what the victims were doing in eternity. A gentle breeze left the room and her head filled with bittersweet thankfulness and the residual energy of the Titanic.

Debbie actually witnessed the papers in her trash can being compressed. The noise of all the papers momentarily distracted her and she had to ask for quiet from the young man.

"Why did he smush your paper trash down," I asked.

"Because he could," said Debbie.

"The spirits in the vision were enjoying a summer day?" I puzzled.

"Yes, they were and they can."

"You were not frightened looking over the side of the ship?"

"No. I was so totally humbled by being aboard that I was not afraid until he took me in that whirlwind. I agreed to participate in his visions, but not to endanger myself. He definitely wanted this world to know we did not seduce the spirits. No spells. No witchcraft. This story is their unadulterated story. This is the story he taught me to teach others:"

Memories can be torturous or amazing to a human soul. We can capture a loved one's smile and photograph it into the subconscious for safe keeping. We can simply memorize the lines of a poem to keep it with us. We can remember something as delightful as a laugh or bury something as horrific as an accident in the recesses of our mind. We can all share our memories with others.

This young man said that memories can be warm and loving, but can also resonate a difficult reality. The person holding the hard memory can release that memory to another who will feel the same pain, but by releasing can free both inhabitants, physical or spiritual. The end result, what matters most, is an emotional connection.

By inviting another to share, we can learn so much, personal and integrative, from either the living or the passed. It is an honor to be asked to listen in trust with obligation, understanding and respect for a perspective that becomes another and another until it thrives eternally. A memory has no boundary, no rules. It is a sanctuary owned by one until it is shared, making it amazing and torturous holding something so powerful with no end, even on the Other Side.

EPILOGUE

I t was early afternoon after a hearty lunch of pasta and broccoli and lots of writing and Debbie decided to watch television in her bedroom while putting away a basket filled with clean laundry. The last chapter, or what we believed to be the last chapter, was finished. The time had come to honor the Titanic by finally seeing the movie and she was going to do just that.

"Whoever wants to join in and watch the movie with me, feel free. Come on over." The words came out loud from her. Within minutes, others were in the room. She counted the orbs flying about as she put away five pairs of stockings into the night stand to tend to the last of the clothing. Grabbing a few bed pillows to place behind her back that still ached from writing the chapter about the little girl, she wore warm socks, had her water bottle and tucked her afghan about her. As she watched the movie, she realized how amazing it was she was able to experience what she had done on the Titanic.

She looked over toward the right where her closet was located. It served as the vortex or entrance for spirits. She counted the orbs flying about and asked them to keep still so they and she could enjoy the movie. Smiling, she saw a man with black boots enter behind four others whom she had not met during the writing of the book.

The Man in the Black Boots smiled from a bright light above her hope chest. He watched the movie, gaping at the flat screen television. Silent for a long time, he then realized that they captured the essence of the disaster. Those in the room with him agreed as they watched the Titanic plow through the ocean.

"Looks just like it, eh?" One of the men commented.

A young woman agreed with a nod and the others followed suit.

"Sorrow is here," said the young Italian who added that no one present was holding a grudge. He winked at Debbie to let her know it was okay for them all to be watching together. She watched four of them leave, one by one, vanishing to another place.

Standing alone, each comfortable with a friend, one in the physical world, one in the Other Side, they fell deep into watching the movie. She watched the Titanic story unfold, completely beginning to feel at peace. Her back ache disappeared as her spirit friend did, too.

AFTERWORD

The soul purpose in writing this book was to validate the lives and deaths of the victims of the sinking of the Titanic. The mere suggestion immediately brought the spirits. Except for flashes in form or voices, they appear chronologically for the most part to portent their intentions. We wrote as they came, not choosing in order of the wealthiest or most interesting, but first come, first serve. We had no divine outline, but they appeared as if we did, eclectic in their social genre and nationalities.

Our purpose is genuine, not one coming from egos about what we could reveal. The psychic medium was with them on the Other Side. They were here with us in unscheduled or intentional visits. None shared their full identity and we did not contaminate any information from the voices of the Titanic by studying data or statistics. What little executed research was for confirmation, not too embellish the known facts.

Our Man in the Shiny Black Boots basically wrote the ending of this book in a final vision in which he emphatically declared we were to include the information in it. Neither one of us could have said it better. When Debbie sent me the last of the text, including the epilogue, several empty pages followed—a sign that we were done in a story that has no end, really. Approximately 1500 people died on the Titanic. Only a few have spoken here, a few intentional spirits some, who after a century, can now rest in peace among those who still do not. Waiting their turn, they continue to come to Debbie with the stories of how they lived and how they died, more stories to be told when the time is right.

Bonnie Meroth

ABOUT THE AUTHORS

Bonnie Meroth has spent nearly thirty years as a multi-media journalist, travel writer, and contributor to magazines, newspapers international publications, travel guides, textbooks, and television networks. She lives in Epping, New Hampshire, where she enjoys being a justice of the peace and notary public while running her public relations and marketing company.

Debbie Raymond is a psychic medium dedicated to communicating with those on the other side and those in the physical world. She opens her mind and spirit, seeing past, present, and future for answers and positive connections as teacher and confidante. She lives in Raymond, New Hampshire, where she enjoys writing, camping, and reading good books.